A

SAINSBURY COOKBOOK

The
FutureCooks
Recipe Book

Selected Recipes
from the Competition

Contents

Published exclusively for J Sainsbury plc
Stamford House Stamford Street
London SE1 9LL
by Martin Books
Simon & Schuster Consumer Group
Fitzwilliam House 32 Trumpington Street
Cambridge CB2 1QY

First published 1991

ISBN 0 85941 764 6

Photographs and illustrations © J Sainsbury plc 1991
Copyright in the recipes lies with the various
authors and publishers (see page 96)

All rights reserved. No part of this publication may be
reproduced, stored in a retrieval system or transmitted, in
any form or by any means, electronic, mechanical,
photocopying or otherwise, without the prior permission
of the copyright holders.

Introduction

Formerly known as Sainsbury's Young Cook of Britain, the FutureCooks competition is an annual event. In this book you will find recipes created by the FutureCooks finalists in 1991. Initially, children between the ages of nine and 15 were asked to create a meal for a favourite celebrity cook. We have selected some of those recipes and have asked each 'favourite' cook to send us a recipe for a starter chosen to suit the young cook and his or her menu.

The competition, which aims to encourage children to take an interest in good food and home cooking, amidst the constant rush of life and swing to 'fast food', was founded 10 years ago, when it received 300 entries. Now, in 1991, the Sainsbury's FutureCooks Awards attract 30,000 entries. With a first prize of a trip to Walt Disney World, and runners-up prizes including a weekend at a top London hotel and a cookery and activity summer holiday, it is not surprising that the competition is a popular one.

At the regional finals of the competition, the children have to prepare their two courses, the main course and a pudding, for two people, in 75 minutes. However, while they are cooking, they are also being interviewed by radio, television and news journalists as well as being questioned by the judges. They also have to cope with being in a totally strange environment and kitchen rather than the familiar surroundings and safe domain of their own homes. How these young cooks are to be admired. The youngsters show true professionalism, a calmness and deftness which is a lesson to us all – there are no tears or hysterics when things don't go quite as they should. Of the eight regional winners featured in this book, one will be selected as overall winner at a national final to be held at The Savoy Hotel. The winner in 1990 was Gill Nutter, from Prestwich, Manchester. Her winning recipes are on pages 93 and 94.

One judge commented that "Every meal prepared here today would be a credit to any top restaurant". I think that sums up the essence of the competition and the competitors. We wish them all every success and thank them for giving us all such good food to eat and to remember them by.

What inspiration and fun we have found. These recipes are the result.

Sainsbury's FutureCooks
Anna Best and Peta Brown,
Chichester, April 1991

Cook's Notes

All recipes serve two unless otherwise stated. Ingredients are given in both metric and imperial measures; use either set of quantities, but not both, in any one recipe. All tablespoons and teaspoons are level unless otherwise stated. Use medium (size 3) eggs unless otherwise stated.

South of England
Winning Recipes by Caroline Godsmark

Guest Cook Carol Godsmark

Oriental Fish Pie (page 6)

Duck Breast
and Lentil Salad
(page 8)

Lemon Grass Creams
(page 7)

Oriental Fish Pie

Caroline Godsmark

4 oz (125 g) fine French beans, topped and tailed

2 small carrots, thinly sliced

4 oz (125 g) salmon fillet

4 oz (125 g) cod fillet

¼ pint (150 ml) milk

4 large shelled scallops, cleaned and sliced in half

1 oz (25 g) butter

½ oz (15 g) plain flour

¼ pint (142 ml) carton single cream

¼ teaspoon crushed dried chillies

¼ teaspoon ground star anise

4 saffron strands, soaked briefly in a few drops of hot water

2 teaspoons finely chopped fresh parsley

4 oz (125 g) puff pastry, thawed if frozen

1 egg, beaten

salt and pepper, to taste

1 Preheat the oven to Gas Mark 7/220°C/425°F. Blanch the beans and carrots in boiling water, then drain.

2 Arrange the salmon and cod in a shallow oven-proof dish and season well with salt and pepper. Pour over the milk and cook in the oven for 10 minutes, adding the scallops for the last minute. Pour off the cooking liquid and reserve. Flake the fish into fairly large pieces, removing skin and bones.

3 To make the sauce, melt the butter in a saucepan, stir in the flour, then gradually add the reserved fish cooking liquid, stirring well after each addition. When all the liquid is incorporated, slowly add the cream and season to taste with salt and pepper. Add the chillies and star anise and cook for 1 minute.

4 Add the saffron to the sauce and simmer very gently for 5 minutes. Strain into a bowl, add the parsley and blanched vegetables, then check the seasoning.

5 Place the cooked fish in a buttered pie dish and pour over the sauce. Leave to cool.

6 Roll out the pastry on a lightly floured surface and use to cover the pie. Flute or crimp the edges and brush with beaten egg. Cook in the oven for 10 minutes or until the pastry is golden, then lower the oven temperature to Gas Mark 4/180°C/350°F and cook the pie for a further 10 minutes.

Lemon Grass Creams

Caroline Godsmark

½ oz (15 g) lemon grass

7 fl oz (200 ml) milk

3 egg yolks

1½ oz (40 g) caster sugar

fresh herbs, to decorate

1 Preheat the oven to Gas Mark 3/160°C/325°F.

2 Crush the lemon grass with the flat side of a heavy knife to release the flavour, then cut into pieces. Put in a saucepan with the milk, bring just to the boil, then remove from the heat and leave to infuse for 15 minutes.

3 Meanwhile, beat the egg yolks with the sugar until light and fluffy. Stir in the warm milk. Strain this custard mixture into a jug and pour into two small ovenproof pots or ramekins. Cover with foil.

4 Set the pots in a roasting tin lined with newspaper and pour in enough hot water to come halfway up the sides of the pots. Heat gently on the hob until the water is almost simmering, then transfer to the oven and cook for 35–40 minutes or until almost set and a knife inserted in the centre comes out clean. Do not let the water boil or the creams will curdle.

5 Take the creams out of the water bath, leave to cool, then refrigerate until required. Allow to come to room temperature before serving decorated with fresh herbs.

'My choice of menu would suit my guest cook, Carol Godsmark, because she has travelled in the Far East and enjoys unusual tastes such as star anise and lemon grass, and she is really fond of fish. She loves light meals and likes food to look colourful. I'd like to give her a good glass of wine with her meal – she's really mega!'

Duck Breast and Lentil Salad

Carol Godsmark

1 boned duck breast (*magret*), weighing about 6–7 oz (175–200 g), skinned

1 carrot, finely diced

1 red onion, finely diced

3 garlic cloves, finely diced

1 inch (2.5 cm) piece fresh root ginger, peeled and finely diced

1 tablespoon soy sauce

6 tablespoons olive oil

2 tablespoons balsamic vinegar

¼ pint (150 ml) red wine

few sprigs fresh thyme

few sprigs fresh marjoram

few sprigs fresh parsley

3 oz (75 g) green lentils, rinsed

2 tablespoons chopped fresh chives

sea salt and freshly ground black pepper, to taste

For the Vinaigrette

2 tablespoons walnut oil

1 tablespoon white wine vinegar

salt and pepper, to taste

1 Remove any excess fat from the duck breast and score the flesh with a sharp knife. Place in an earthenware dish and sprinkle with half the diced vegetables, garlic and ginger.

2 Whisk together the soy sauce, olive oil, balsamic vinegar and red wine and pour over the duck. Add a few sprigs of thyme and leave to marinate for at least 45 minutes.

3 Make a bouquet garni by tying together sprigs of fresh thyme, marjoram and parsley. Put the lentils in a saucepan, cover with water, add ½ teaspoon sea salt and the bouquet garni, bring to the boil and simmer for 10 minutes.

4 To make the walnut oil vinaigrette, beat the ingredients together in a small bowl or jug.

5 Add the remaining diced vegetables and ginger to the lentils and cook for 5–10 minutes or until the vegetables are just tender, adding more water if necessary. Drain well, then discard the bouquet garni and add 2 table-spoons vinaigrette. Toss well, then spread out on a plate and leave to cool. Preheat the grill to high.

6 Remove the duck from the marinade and pat dry. Sprinkle the unfatty side with sea salt and season with freshly ground pepper. Cook under the grill for 5 minutes on each side or until the fat is charred and crisp. Remove from the heat and leave to rest for 5–10 minutes.

7 Meanwhile, toss the lentils in more vinaigrette, if necessary. Add the chopped chives and check the seasoning. Divide between two serving plates.

8 To serve, slice the duck thinly and arrange on the plates next to the lentils.

Caroline Godsmark is 12 years old and lives in Petworth, West Sussex, where her parents own a restaurant. She attends the Great Ballard School in Eartham, near Chichester.

Caroline chose to cook her meal of Oriental Fish Pie, followed by Lemon Grass Creams, for her mother, Carol Godsmark. Not surprisingly, Caroline was taught to cook by her mother but her career aspirations lie in the field of modern dance. When she is not busy in the kitchen, Caroline enjoys sport, travel, fashion and spending time with family and friends.

Carol Godsmark was born in Canada and, after commencing her education there, subsequently attended schools in Czechoslovakia, Switzerland, Denmark and, finally, England. Her varied career has included nursing, advertising, catering and five years as a stewardess with BOAC. She opened her first restaurant in 1985 and her present restaurant, Soanes (in Petworth, West Sussex), in 1987. Carol has travelled extensively throughout the world, sampling a wide variety of cuisines, and is a keen collector of both travel and cookery books.

Chicken Satay with Peanut Sauce

Kerry Hart (12) from Camberley

12 oz (375 g) chicken breast fillets, skinned and cut into ¾ inch (2 cm) cubes

frisée, to garnish

For the Marinade

½ small onion, sliced

1 fl oz (25 ml) groundnut oil

½ teaspoon coriander seeds, crushed

¼ teaspoon fennel seeds, crushed

1 cardamom pod, crushed

1 allspice berry, crushed

¼ teaspoon garam masala

pinch of salt

finely pared rind and juice of ½ lemon

For the Peanut Sauce

1 tablespoon groundnut oil

1 small onion, finely diced

1 garlic clove, crushed

1 oz (25 g) fresh root ginger, peeled and grated

4 oz (125 g) crunchy peanut butter

¼ pint (150 ml) chicken stock

2 oz (50 g) creamed coconut

juice of ½ lime

salt and pepper, to taste

carrot slivers, to garnish

1 To make the marinade, mix together the onion, groundnut oil, coriander, fennel, cardamom, allspice, garam masala and salt. Finely slice the lemon rind and add to the marinade with the lemon juice.

2 Put the chicken into a bowl and pour the marinade over the top. Cover with clingfilm and leave to marinate in the fridge overnight.

3 Remove the chicken cubes and onion from the marinade with a slotted spoon. Reserve the marinade and onion and thread the chicken cubes on to satay sticks or small skewers.

4 To make the peanut sauce, heat the oil in a heavy-based saucepan. Add the onion, garlic and ginger and fry over a low heat for 5 minutes or until soft. Add the peanut butter, chicken stock and creamed coconut and cook, stirring constantly, until blended.

5 Liquidise the sauce in a blender or food processor, then return it to the saucepan. Add the lime juice and season to taste with salt and pepper.

6 Heat the barbecue or grill to high and cook the chicken for 12 minutes, turning once and basting with the reserved marinade. Meanwhile, reheat the sauce gently, then pour into a warmed sauceboat and garnish with carrot slivers.

7 Transfer the kebabs to a warmed serving platter, scatter the reserved marinated onion over the top and garnish with frisée. Serve immediately with the warm peanut sauce.

Casserole of Duck Breasts with Raspberries

Diana Frewing (13) from Portsmouth

2 boned duck breasts

1 teaspoon virgin olive oil

½ carrot, peeled and minced

½ onion, minced

3 fl oz (75 ml) dessert wine

3 fl oz (75 ml) home-made stock (preferably duck)

bouquet garni

1½ tablespoons redcurrant jelly

2 teaspoons lemon juice

6 oz (175 g) raspberries

salt and pepper, to taste

1 Preheat the oven to Gas Mark 6/200°C/400°F.

2 Season the duck breasts well with salt and pepper. Prick the breasts all over with a skewer and place, skin side up, on a wire rack in a roasting tin. Cook in the oven for 15 minutes.

3 Drain the fat that comes out of the duck into a flameproof casserole. Add the olive oil, carrot and onion and fry gently, stirring, for about 3 minutes or until brown.

4 Add the duck to the casserole with the wine, stock and bouquet garni. Cover and simmer for 20 minutes.

5 Meanwhile, spoon the redcurrant jelly into another saucepan and add the lemon juice. Reserve a few of the raspberries for garnish and press the remainder through a nylon sieve into the pan with the lemon juice and redcurrant jelly.

6 When the duck is cooked, lift it out of the pan with a slotted spoon, place on a warmed serving dish and keep warm.

7 Add the duck cooking juices to the raspberry mixture, bring gently to the boil, stirring, then boil rapidly to reduce until thick enough to coat the duck. Spoon over the duck and garnish with the reserved raspberries. Serve with a selection of lightly steamed vegetables glazed with butter.

Blueberry Boats with Lemon Pastry

Tamsin Hirst (14) from Winchester

For the Pastry

5 oz (150 g) plain flour

3 oz (75 g) margarine

½ oz (15 g) ground almonds

1½ oz (40 g) icing sugar

grated rind of 1 lemon

1 egg yolk

1½ tablespoons lemon juice

For the Filling

2½ fl oz (65 ml) natural yogurt

¼ teaspoon grated lemon rind

2 oz (50 g) blueberries

1 tablespoon redcurrant jelly

1 Preheat the oven to Gas Mark 5/190°C/375°F.

2 To make the pastry, sift the flour into a mixing bowl and rub in the margarine until the mixture resembles fine breadcrumbs. Stir in the ground almonds, icing sugar and lemon rind. Beat together the egg yolk and lemon juice, stir into the flour mixture and bind to a smooth dough. Wrap in clingfilm and chill in the fridge for 30 minutes.

3 Roll out the pastry and use to line four 4 inch (10 cm) boat-shaped moulds. Bake in the oven for 12–15 minutes or until golden. Allow to cool slightly, then remove from the tins and leave to cool completely on a wire rack.

4 To make the filling, blend the yogurt with the grated lemon rind and divide between the pastry cases. Arrange the blueberries on top.

5 Melt the redcurrant jelly in a saucepan and brush gently over the blueberries. Allow to set before serving.

Fruit and Coffee Hazelnut Meringue

Sophie Maskey (15) from Shoreham-by-Sea

2 eggs, separated

5 oz (150 g) caster sugar

¼ teaspoon white vinegar

¼ teaspoon vanilla essence

2 oz (50 g) hazelnuts, roasted and chopped

1 oz (25 g) cornflour

½ pint (300 ml) evaporated milk

1 teaspoon instant coffee powder

seasonal fruits, to decorate

1 Preheat the oven to Gas Mark 4/180°C/350°F. Grease, flour and line an 8 inch (20 cm) sandwich tin, using baking parchment.

2 Whisk the egg whites until stiff. Whisk in 2 oz (50 g) of the caster sugar, then carefully fold in a further 2 oz (50 g) sugar, the vinegar and vanilla. Fold in the hazelnuts.

3 Turn the meringue mixture into the prepared tin, spread evenly and bake in the oven for 35–40 minutes or until crisp and dry. Remove from the tin, leave to cool, then carefully peel off the baking parchment.

4 Blend the cornflour with a little of the milk in a saucepan. Add the remaining milk and bring to the boil, stirring constantly, until thick and glossy.

5 Remove the pan from the heat and beat in the egg yolks, coffee and remaining sugar. Pour into a bowl, cover the surface with damp greaseproof paper and leave to cool.

6 To serve, place the meringue on a flat serving plate and spread the coffee cream on top. Decorate with fruit.

Prune and Port Fool

James Carreras (14) from Eastleigh

2 oz (50 g) stoned prunes,
soaked overnight

2 tablespoons port

grated rind and juice of
1 orange

1 oz (25 g) caster sugar

2½ fl oz (65 ml) double cream

2½ fl oz (65 ml) thick custard

orange twists, to decorate

1 Drain the prunes and put in a saucepan with the port, orange rind and juice and sugar. Simmer for 15 minutes, then leave to cool slightly.

2 Purée the prunes in a blender or food processor, transfer to a bowl and leave to cool completely.

3 Whip the cream until stiff, then fold into the prune purée with the custard. Chill until required, then spoon into individual bowls or glasses and serve decorated with orange twists.

Salade de Vicaire (Curate's Salad)

This simple starter by Albert Roux was especially chosen by him to serve before Diana Frewing's rich Casserole of Duck Breasts with Raspberries (page 11). Diana chose Albert, well known proprietor of London's Le Gavroche restaurant, as her guest cook because she admires his skills of pâtisserie.

Serves Six

1 full-hearted lettuce

½ frisée

1 small radicchio

10 bunches lamb's lettuce (corn salad)

18 slices French bread

1 garlic clove

8 oz (250 g) smoked bacon, in one piece

⅔ teaspoon Dijon mustard

juice of ½ lemon

2 tablespoons wine vinegar

1 fl oz (25 ml) olive oil

3 fl oz (75 ml) groundnut oil

1½ tablespoons cider vinegar

3 hard-boiled egg yolks, sieved or finely chopped

salt and pepper, to taste

1 Trim, wash and dry the salad leaves.

2 Toast the bread under the grill or in the oven until dry and golden brown, then rub with the garlic clove.

3 Remove the rind and slice the bacon evenly. Cut the slices into thin sticks (*lardons*), put in a saucepan and cover with water. Bring to the boil and boil for 2 minutes, then remove from the heat and drain. Refresh with cold water, then drain again.

4 Put the mustard, lemon juice and wine vinegar in a large salad bowl and mix together. Stir in the olive and groundnut oils and season to taste with salt and pepper. Add the salad leaves and toss well.

5 Put the *lardons* in a frying pan and sauté in their own fat over a high heat until pale golden. Pour the *lardons* and their fat on to the salad.

6 Pour the cider vinegar into the frying pan and bring to the boil, stirring to scrape any bacon pieces off the bottom of the pan. Boil for 1 minute or until the vinegar is reduced by half, then pour over the salad.

7 Quickly toss everything in the salad bowl together, then arrange the French bread *croûtons* on top and scatter over the hard-boiled egg yolks. Serve immediately.

East of England
Winning Recipes by Marcus Croskell

Guest Cook Michel Roux

Omelette à l'Oseille (page 20)

Moules Marinière (page 18)

Ginger Syllabub (page 19)

Moules Marinière

Marcus Croskell

1 small onion, finely chopped

2 garlic cloves, finely chopped

4 sprigs fresh parsley

1 bay leaf

¼ teaspoon chopped fresh thyme

2 oz (50 g) butter

½ pint (300 ml) dry white wine

2 lb (1 kg) mussels, scrubbed and soaked

2 tablespoons single cream

freshly ground black pepper, to taste

4 tablespoons chopped fresh parsley, to garnish

1 Put the onion, garlic, herbs, butter and pepper to taste in a large saucepan. Pour in the wine, bring to the boil and boil for 2–3 minutes to evaporate the alcohol and reduce the amount of liquid slightly.

2 Add the mussels to the pan, cover tightly and boil rapidly over a high heat for about 5 minutes or until the mussels are cooked and the shells have opened. Shake the pan frequently during cooking to toss the mussels and ensure even cooking.

3 Using a slotted spoon, lift the mussels out of the cooking liquid, transfer to a large warmed tureen and keep warm. Discard any mussels that have not opened.

4 Leave the cooking liquid to stand for a moment to allow any sand from the mussels to settle on the bottom of the pan. Remove the parsley and bay leaf. Add a little cream to the liquid and ladle over the mussels, being careful not to disturb any sediment at the bottom of the pan. Sprinkle with chopped parsley and serve immediately with wholemeal bread and a dressed green salad.

Ginger Syllabub

Marcus Croskell

2 pieces stem ginger, finely chopped

2 tablespoons stem ginger syrup

2 tablespoons medium or dry sherry

1 oz (25 g) caster sugar

¼ pint (142 ml) carton double cream

1 oz (25 g) crystallised ginger, chopped, to decorate

1 Put the stem ginger and syrup, sherry and sugar in a bowl and stir to combine.

2 Whip the cream until thick, then fold in the ginger mixture until evenly distributed throughout the cream. Cover and chill in the fridge for several hours.

3 Just before serving, whip the syllabub again, then spoon into two individual glasses. Decorate with chopped crystallised ginger.

'I really think that Michel Roux would enjoy my menu because I saw him and Albert Roux on television creating new recipes using mussels. They both agreed, however, that their favourite mussel dish was "as Mama made them", that is Moules Marinière. Hence my choice of mussels as a special tempting ingredient – they are delicious!'

Omelette à l'Oseille (Sorrel Omelette)

Michel Roux

3 oz (75 g) sorrel

1½ oz (40 g) butter

4 fl oz (125 ml) double cream

pinch of grated nutmeg

6 eggs

1 teaspoon oil

1 tablespoon grated Gruyère cheese

salt and pepper, to taste

1 Preheat the grill to high.

2 Remove the stalks from the sorrel and wash and dry the leaves. Roll up each leaf like a cigar and snip finely into shreds.

3 Put the sorrel in a sauté pan with ½ oz (15 g) butter, cover tightly and cook gently until all the water from the sorrel has evaporated. Remove from the heat.

4 Whip the cream until the whisk leaves a trail when lifted. Season to taste with salt and a pinch of nutmeg.

5 Break the eggs into a bowl and beat with a fork. Season to taste with salt and pepper.

6 Put the oil in an omelette pan or small frying pan with the remaining butter and heat until the fat sizzles. Pour in the beaten eggs and cook, stirring gently with a fork, until the omelette sets and is almost cooked. Spread the sorrel across the centre, then fold over the omelette.

7 Roll the omelette on to a heatproof serving plate. Cover with cream and sprinkle with grated cheese. Place immediately under the hot grill for 2–3 minutes or until the cheese has melted and turned pale golden. Serve at once.

Marcus Croskell, aged 11, lives in Ipswich, Suffolk, and attends St. Joseph's School, Oakhill.

Marcus was taught to cook by his mother and grandfather. He also enjoys skiing, squash, swimming, cricket and badminton. He is planning to train as an architect when he leaves school.

Born in France, Michel Roux began his apprenticeship at the Pâtisserie Loyal in Paris, then spent two years as *commis pâtissier cuisinier* at the British Embassy in Paris. He later spent six years as chef to Cécile de Rothschild.

The opening of Le Gavroche in London in 1967 was followed by a number of other restaurants, including the Waterside Inn in Berkshire in 1972. Run by Michel, the restaurant has been awarded three rosettes by the Michelin Guide.

In conjunction with his brother, Albert, Michel has published three books and made many television appearances, most notably in the Roux brothers' own series, Cooking at Home with the Rouxs.

Devilled Crab

Sara Thomas (14) from Billericay

½ oz (15 g) butter

½ oz (15 g) plain flour

2 fl oz (50 ml) milk

2 fl oz (50 ml) single cream

pinch of grated nutmeg

pinch of mustard powder

1 egg yolk

2 fl oz (50 ml) sherry

8 oz (250 g) crab meat

breadcrumbs

salt and pepper, to taste

lemon wedges, to garnish

1 Preheat the oven to Gas Mark 6/200°C/400°F.

2 Melt the butter, add the flour and stir with a whisk until blended. Bring the milk and cream to the boil. Add, all at once, to the butter and flour and heat gently, whisking until smooth. Stir in the nutmeg and mustard.

3 Add a little of the hot sauce to the egg yolk and beat lightly. Add to the sauce in the pan and heat gently, stirring, until thickened. Add the sherry and crab meat and season.

4 Spoon the mixture into two cleaned crab shells, if available, two 4 oz (125 g) capacity ovenproof ramekin dishes or one baking dish. Sprinkle with breadcrumbs and bake for about 10 minutes or until browned. Serve with lemon wedges.

Seafood Fillo Parcels

Kate Anderson (10) from Aslacton

½ onion, sliced

8 fl oz (250 ml) milk

2 fl oz (50 ml) white wine

½ teaspoon dried mixed herbs

1 teaspoon chopped fresh
parsley

4 oz (125 g) salmon

4 oz (125 g) cod

3 oz (75 g) butter

1 tablespoon plain flour

2 oz (50 g) peeled cooked
prawns

6 sheets fillo pastry, about
13 × 7 inches (32 × 18 cm),
thawed if frozen

salt and pepper, to taste

1 Preheat the oven to Gas Mark 6/200°C/400°F.

2 Put the onion in a saucepan with the milk, wine and herbs. Add the salmon and cod and bring to the boil. Simmer for 8–10 minutes or until the fish is tender. Remove the fish and set aside. Strain and reserve the cooking liquid. Flake the fish, removing any skin and bones.

3 Melt 1 oz (25 g) butter in a saucepan. Add the flour and cook gently, stirring, for 1–2 minutes. Remove from the heat and gradually blend in the reserved cooking liquid. Bring to the boil, stirring continuously, until thick. Gently stir in the fish and prawns. Season to taste, then leave to cool.

4 Melt the remaining butter and use to brush over three sheets of fillo pastry. Pile the sheets one on top of the other and spread half the fish mixture along the bottom edge. Fold over the pastry sides and roll into a pancake shape. Repeat with the remaining pastry and fish mixture to make a second parcel.

5 Place the parcels on a greased baking sheet with the joins underneath and brush with melted butter. Cook in the oven for 15–20 minutes or until golden. Serve hot with lightly boiled or steamed samphire.

Chocolate Dessert Cups

Jeremy Watkins (11) from Brentwood

3 oz (75 g) plain chocolate

¼ oz (10 g) butter

2 eggs, separated

2 teaspoons brandy

2 teaspoons coffee essence

1 Break up the chocolate and put in a heatproof bowl with the butter. Place over a saucepan of hot, not boiling, water and heat gently, stirring, until melted.

2 Remove from the heat and beat in the egg yolks, brandy and coffee essence.

3 Whisk the egg whites until stiff, then fold into the chocolate mixture. Pour into small cups or ramekin dishes and leave in a cool place until set. Chill in the fridge until ready to serve.

Salmon and Asparagus with Dill Sauce

Tim Barrett-Jolley (13) from Haddenham

2 egg yolks

4 tablespoons melted butter

1 teaspoon lemon juice

¼ teaspoon prepared mild mustard

pinch of sugar

1 tablespoon chopped fresh dill

2 tablespoons single cream

2 salmon cutlets

½–¾ pint (300–450 ml) fish stock

1 bunch young asparagus, trimmed

salt and pepper, to taste

1 To make the sauce, put the egg yolks in a heatproof bowl and beat in the butter, lemon juice and mustard. Place over a saucepan of hot water and beat until thick and creamy.

2 Transfer the sauce to a food processor and add the sugar, dill and salt and pepper to taste. Process until very smooth, adding a little cream until the consistency is correct. Transfer to a saucepan.

3 Put the fish in another saucepan, just cover with stock and poach gently for about 4 minutes or until tender. Remove the fish from the stock and carefully remove the skin. Place the fish on a warmed serving plate and keep warm.

4 Arrange the asparagus stems in a circle on a flat microwave-proof plate, with their tips towards the centre. Add a little water, cover and microwave on HIGH (100%) for 5–6 minutes. (Alternatively, steam the asparagus or simmer gently in a little water for 5–10 minutes.) Drain, season to taste and arrange on the plate with the salmon.

5 Reheat the sauce gently, without boiling, and pour a generous amount between the fish and the asparagus. Serve immediately with boiled new potatoes.

Coconut Pudding

Susan Alliott (14) from Thetford

½ pint (300 ml) creamy milk

1½ oz (40 g) caster sugar

1 oz (25 g) unsalted butter

2 oz (50 g) creamed coconut

½ oz (15 g) sultanas

1 tablespoon rosewater

1 oz (25 g) flaked almonds, toasted, to decorate

1 Bring the milk and sugar to the boil, then set aside.

2 Melt the butter in a saucepan and blend in the creamed coconut. Cook gently for 5 minutes. Add the milk mixture and continue cooking over a low heat, stirring continuously, for 10–15 minutes or until reduced by half. Add the sultanas and rosewater.

3 Transfer the mixture to two ramekin dishes, leave to cool, then chill until the consistency of thick cream. Decorate with almonds.

Tartare of Marinated Wild
Salmon with Cucumber Salad
(page 28)

Honey Wafers with
Mascarpone Cream and
Berries (page 27)

Midlands

Winning Recipes by Gregory Lewis

Guest Cook Raymond Blanc

Roast Rack of Lamb with Wine
and Shallot Sauce (page 26)

Roast Rack of Lamb with Wine and Shallot Sauce

Gregory Lewis

small rack of lamb (6 cutlets), well trimmed

For the Rösti

1 inch (2.5 cm) piece fresh root ginger, peeled and grated

1 large potato, peeled and grated

1 oz (25 g) fresh horseradish, peeled and grated

5 tablespoons butter, melted

salt and pepper, to taste

For the Sauce

7 fl oz (200 ml) red wine

5 shallots, finely chopped

sprig fresh thyme

½ bay leaf

1 fl oz (25 ml) port

1 fl oz (25 ml) red wine vinegar

¼ pint (150 ml) beef stock

2 fl oz (50 ml) chicken stock

½ oz (15 g) butter

1 Preheat the oven to Gas Mark 5/190°C/375°F. Place the rack of lamb in a roasting tin and roast in the oven for about 20 minutes.

2 Meanwhile, to make the rösti, put the ginger in a small saucepan, cover with water, bring to the boil, then simmer for 5 minutes. Drain, refresh with cold water, then drain again.

3 Put the grated potato in a piece of muslin and squeeze out all the moisture. Turn the potato into a bowl and add the ginger, horseradish and salt and pepper to taste. Stir in 1½ tablespoons melted butter.

4 Heat the remaining butter in a frying pan and place two crumpet rings in the pan. Divide the potato mixture between the rings, pressing down firmly. Cook for about 10 minutes or until the underside is golden brown, then remove the rings, turn the röstis and cook until brown on the other side.

5 Meanwhile, to make the sauce, put the wine, shallots, thyme, bay leaf, port and vinegar in a saucepan. Bring to the boil and boil rapidly until reduced by two thirds. Add the beef and chicken stock and boil again until reduced by half. Gradually blend in the butter. Remove the herbs.

6 To serve, divide the rack of lamb into cutlets and arrange on a bed of potato röstis on a warmed serving plate. Pour a little

of the sauce over the cutlets and serve the remainder in a warmed sauceboat. Serve the lamb with crisp julienne of leeks and seasonal baby vegetables.

Honey Wafers with Mascarpone Cream and Berries

Gregory Lewis

1 tablespoon unsalted butter, softened

¾ oz (20 g) icing sugar, sifted

1 tablespoon clear honey

¾ oz (20 g) plain flour, sifted

1 egg white

½ teaspoon ground cinnamon

4 oz (125 g) wild strawberries, hulled

4 oz (125 g) raspberries

icing sugar, to dredge

mint leaves or strawberry flowers, to decorate

For the Mascarpone Cream

1 egg yolk

1 tablespoon caster sugar

1 tablespoon Mascarpone cheese

1 teaspoon Amaretto liqueur

1 Preheat the oven to Gas Mark 7/220°C/425°F. Line a baking sheet with baking parchment.

2 Cream the butter until very soft, then gradually add the icing sugar, honey, flour, egg white and cinnamon, whisking well after each addition.

3 Put 1–2 teaspoons mixture on to the lined baking sheet. Moisten the back of the spoon and spread the mixture to form a very thin round about 3 inches (7 cm) in diameter. Repeat to make six rounds, spacing them 1–2 inches (2.5–5 cm) apart.

4 Bake in the oven for about 3 minutes or until golden brown. Carefully remove the wafers from the baking parchment and cool on a wire rack.

5 To make the Mascarpone cream, beat the egg yolk and sugar together until pale and thick. Mix in the cheese and beat again. Stir in the liqueur. Place in the fridge until well chilled.

6 To assemble, spread two wafers with Mascarpone cream. Place on two serving plates and arrange strawberries and raspberries on top. Spread two more wafers with cream and place on top of the fruit. Cover with the remaining fruit and top with the final wafers. Dredge with icing sugar and decorate.

'Raymond Blanc is renowned for the fresh taste and lightness of his food and for his superb presentation. Within the limitations of time and budget, I have chosen to use high quality, fresh ingredients, balancing the richness of the wine sauce with the freshness of the young vegetables. My special ingredients are the horseradish and ginger in the rosti. I think these give the rosti an interesting flavour which complements the lamb. The dessert is light, crisp and not too creamy.'

Tartare of Marinated Wild Salmon with Cucumber Salad

Raymond Blanc

4 oz (125 g) salmon fillet (preferably wild), skinned

1 teaspoon salt

1 teaspoon caster sugar

a little freshly grated lemon rind

1 teaspoon chopped fresh dill

½ teaspoon soured cream

Dijon mustard

lemon juice

pepper, to taste

For the Cucumber Salad

1 inch (2.5 cm) piece cucumber

¼ teaspoon salt

¼ teaspoon white wine vinegar

½ tablespoon non-scented oil (such as groundnut, grapeseed or sunflower oil)

pepper, to taste

To Garnish

wafer-thin lemon segments

1 tablespoon soured cream

sprigs fresh dill

1 teaspoon caviar, salmon eggs or lumpfish roe, chilled (optional)

1 Gently remove any stray bones from the salmon and place on a piece of clingfilm large enough to enclose it completely.

2 In a bowl, mix together the salt, sugar, lemon rind and chopped dill and rub gently into both sides of the salmon. Fold the clingfilm over and seal like a parcel. Leave to marinate in the fridge for 12 hours.

3 Unwrap the salmon, rinse under cold running water and pat dry with absorbent paper. Cut the salmon into ⅛ inch (3 mm) cubes and place in a bowl. Put the soured cream in a separate bowl and season with a little mustard, lemon juice and pepper. Mix in the salmon cubes and leave in a cool place for 1 hour.

4 Meanwhile, to make the cucumber salad, peel the cucumber, halve lengthways and scoop out the seeds with a teaspoon. Slice finely, place in a sieve and sprinkle with salt. Leave for 30 minutes.

5 Rinse the cucumber under cold running water, pat dry and place in a small bowl. Add the wine vinegar, oil and pepper to taste and mix thoroughly.

6 Arrange the salmon mixture and salad on two serving plates and garnish with wafer-thin lemon segments, soured cream, tiny sprigs of dill and caviar, if liked.

Gregory (Greg) Lewis is 15 and lives in Nuneaton, Warwickshire. He attends the Dixie Grammar School at Market Bosworth.

Apart from cooking, Greg's interests include tennis and radio-controlled car racing. He is taking Home Economics at school but his parents have also been involved in teaching him to cook. He has not yet made a decision about his future career.

Raymond Blanc is chef and proprietor of the world-famous restaurant and hotel, Le Manoir aux Quat' Saisons at Great Milton, Oxford. Raymond began his career working as a waiter in a restaurant and in 1972 came to England to work as a head chef. He opened his first restaurant in 1977 followed by Le Manoir in 1984. Le Manoir is one of only nine hotels in the world to hold the Relais & Château Gold and Red Shields, and has been the recipient of numerous other top awards.

As well as publishing his own book of recipes, *Le Manoir aux Quat' Saisons*, Raymond has contributed to a number of other publications and has made several television appearances, including on the BBC's Food and Drink and Channel 4's Take Six Cooks.

Sauté of Lamb's Liver with Herbs

James Edmondson (11) from Tewkesbury

½ oz (15 g) plain flour

8 oz (250 g) lamb's liver, sliced into thin strips

1 oz (25 g) butter

2 tablespoons chopped fresh parsley

2 tablespoons chopped fresh chives

2 tablespoons chopped fresh tarragon

8 oz (250 g) button mushrooms, finely chopped

salt and pepper, to taste

lemon wedges, to garnish

1 Season the flour with salt and pepper, add the liver and toss until coated.

2 Melt the butter in a frying pan and fry the liver quickly until browned. Add the herbs and mushrooms and stir-fry for a few minutes or until the liver is tender.

3 Garnish with lemon wedges and serve immediately with boiled wild rice and steamed vegetables or a mixed green salad.

Poussin with Fresh Herbs

Clara Warren (12) from Newark

1 oven-ready 'double' poussin

bunch fresh garden herbs, chopped

1 garlic clove, finely chopped

2 tablespoons olive oil

2 teaspoons cornflour

¼ pint (150 ml) chicken stock

¼ pint (150 ml) red wine

salt and pepper, to taste

1 Preheat the oven to Gas Mark 5/190°C/375°F.

2 Cut the poussin in half using poultry shears and push the chopped herbs and garlic under the skin. Place in a roasting tin, brush with olive oil, season and roast in the oven for 30–35 minutes. Transfer to a warmed serving dish and keep warm.

3 Stir the cornflour into the cooking juices in the roasting tin, then blend in the stock and wine. Bring to the boil, stirring continuously until smooth, then pour into a warmed sauceboat.

4 Serve the poussin with the red wine sauce, boiled new potatoes and stir-fried carrots and mange tout.

Turkey with Lime and Tarragon

James Mitchell (10) from Kettering

1 oz (25 g) butter

4 turkey breast escalopes

1 small onion, sliced

3 tablespoons plain flour

½ pint (300 ml) chicken stock

finely grated rind and juice of
2 limes

1 teaspoon chopped fresh
tarragon or ½ teaspoon dried

4 tablespoons natural yogurt
or single cream

salt and pepper, to taste

lime wedges, to garnish

1 Preheat the oven to Gas Mark 4/180°C/350°F.

2 Heat the butter in a shallow flameproof casserole, fry the turkey escalopes until golden, then remove from the pan. Add the onion to the pan and fry until golden.

3 Stir the flour into the pan, then remove from the heat and gradually blend in the stock. Bring slowly to the boil, stirring, then add the lime rind. Strain the lime juice and add to the casserole with the tarragon and salt and pepper to taste.

4 Return the turkey to the casserole, cover and cook in the oven for 45 minutes.

5 Skim any fat from the surface of the casserole and check the seasoning. Put the casserole on the hob, stir in the yogurt or cream and warm through gently, without boiling. Serve immediately, garnished with the lime wedges.

Blackberry Surprise

Timothy Atherton (9) from Solihull

1½ oz (40 g) butter

2 oz (50 g) porridge oats

2 tablespoons light brown soft sugar

4 oz (125 g) blackberries

5 oz (150 g) carton natural yogurt

1 Melt the butter in a saucepan and add the porridge oats and sugar. Heat gently, stirring, until the oats are browned, then leave to cool.

2 Reserve a few blackberries for decoration and put the remainder in a saucepan with a little water. Cover and simmer very gently until just cooked, then cool.

3 Layer the blackberries with the yogurt and oat mixture in two individual serving glasses. Decorate with the reserved blackberries.

Two-fruit Upside-down Tart

Leo Potter (13) from Oxford

1¼ oz (30 g) unsalted butter

1¼ oz (30 g) light soft brown sugar

2 oz (50 g) plain flour

½ oz (15 g) icing sugar

1 egg yolk, beaten

½ tablespoon water

8 oz (250 g) dessert apples

flaked almonds and grapes, to decorate

1 Preheat the oven to Gas Mark 4/180°C/350°F. Line the base of a shallow 5 inch (12 cm) square tin with greaseproof paper. Melt ¼ oz (5 g) butter and brush over the inside of the tin. Sprinkle the brown sugar evenly over the paper and press down.

2 Sift the flour into a bowl and rub in the remaining butter. Sift in the icing sugar and stir in half the egg yolk and the water to bind the mixture to a rough dough. Knead until smooth, then turn on to a lightly floured surface and roll out to roughly the size of the prepared tin. Set aside to rest.

3 Peel, core and thinly slice the apples. Arrange in three neat rows on top of the sugar in the base of the tin. Position the pastry carefully over the apple, press down gently and trim the edges.

4 Bake the tart in the oven for 35–40 minutes or until crisp and golden brown. Leave to cool.

5 Meanwhile, spread the almond flakes on a baking sheet and toast in the oven, turning occasionally, until evenly browned.

6 When the tart is cool, turn it out, upside-down, on to a serving plate. To decorate, halve the grapes, de-seed if necessary, and arrange between the rows of apples, alternating with toasted almonds.

Beignets Soufflés Fromage

**Ruth Mott is well known for her BBC television series, The Victorian Kitchen.
James Mitchell chose her as his guest cook because she likes experimenting
with new ideas and would be interested to sample his Turkey with Lime and
Tarragon (page 31). She suggested this recipe for savoury choux balls as an
ideal starter.**

Serves Four

3¾ oz (105 g) plain flour

1 teaspoon mustard powder

7 fl oz (200 ml) water

3 oz (75 g) unsalted butter

3 eggs, beaten

**2 oz (50 g) Parmesan cheese,
grated**

oil, for deep frying

salt and pepper, to taste

1 Sift together the flour
and mustard powder into
a bowl and season with
salt and pepper.

2 Put the water and butter
in a large saucepan and
cook over a low heat until
the butter has melted,
then bring rapidly to the
boil. Remove from the
heat and tip in all the
seasoned flour at once.
Mix in quickly with a
wooden spoon, then beat
just until the dough is
smooth and comes away
from the sides of the pan.
Allow the mixture to cool
slightly, then beat in the
eggs, a little at a time,
followed by the grated
cheese.

3 Heat the oil in a deep fat
fryer to 160°C/325°F.

4 Using a dessertspoon,
drop spoonfuls of choux
pastry in batches into the
hot oil and fry for 7–10
minutes. Raise the
temperature of the oil to
170°C/338°F for the last
minute or until the
beignets are crisp and
golden.

5 Drain the beignets on
absorbent paper and keep
them warm while frying
the remainder.

Potage Purée de Lentilles
(Old-fashioned Lentil Soup)

This satisfying vegetable soup, by Julia Child, would be best served before a light main course. Julia Child is celebrated throughout the world as one of the leading exponents of French cuisine. Leo Potter devised his menu especially for her because he thought she would appreciate its originality. His Two-Fruit Upside-down Tart is on page 33.

Serves Four to Six

1½ oz (40 g) butter

2 celery sticks, roughly chopped

1 carrot, roughly chopped

1 onion, roughly chopped

1 leek, roughly chopped

3 tablespoons plain flour

2½ pints (1.5 litres) hot stock (ham, poultry, meat or vegetable) or water

1 bay leaf

¼ teaspoon chopped fresh thyme

2 oz (50 g) turnip or swede, diced (optional)

12 oz (375 g) lentils, rinsed

2 teaspoons salt

1 Melt the butter in a large saucepan, stir in the vegetables, cover and cook over a moderately low heat for about 10 minutes or until the vegetables are tender and beginning to brown lightly, stirring occasionally.

2 Blend in the flour and cook for 2 minutes, stirring. Remove the pan from the heat.

3 Gradually blend in 8 fl oz (250 ml) hot stock or water, stirring vigorously. Pour in the remaining stock or water and bring to simmering point, adding the herbs and diced turnip or swede (if using).

4 Stir in the lentils and salt, cover the pan loosely and simmer slowly for 1¼–1½ hours, or until the lentils are very tender.

5 Allow the soup to cool slightly, remove the bay leaf, then purée through a vegetable mill or in an electric blender or food processor. Return to the saucepan and heat gently. Check the seasoning and add a little more hot stock if necessary before serving.

South-West England and Wales

Winning Recipes by Morgan Jones

Guest Cook Franco Taruschio

Potato-wrapped Lamb Fillet
with Orange Sauce
(page 38)

Piedmontese
Peppers (page 40)

Cherry Almond Brûlées
(page 39)

Potato-wrapped Lamb Fillet with Orange Sauce

Morgan Jones

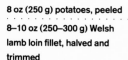

8 oz (250 g) potatoes, peeled

8–10 oz (250–300 g) Welsh lamb loin fillet, halved and trimmed

½ large garlic clove

1 tablespoon olive oil

1 tablespoon chopped fresh rosemary

1 egg, beaten

½ oz (15 g) butter, melted

salt and pepper, to taste

rosemary leaves and orange slices, to garnish

For the Sauce

1 teaspoon cornflour

juice of ½ orange

2½ fl oz (65 ml) lamb stock

1 teaspoon soft brown sugar

1 tablespoon chopped watercress

salt and pepper, to taste

1 Preheat the oven to Gas Mark 4/180°C/350°F.

2 Cook the potatoes in boiling salted water for 8 minutes, drain and cool.

3 Make small, deep incisions all over the meat with a sharp knife. Cut the garlic clove into small

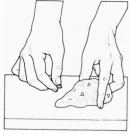

slivers and push one piece into each incision. Brush the meat with olive oil and leave to marinate for a few minutes.

4 Heat a frying pan over a low heat, add the meat and fry until lightly browned on all sides. Remove the meat from the pan and place on a greased baking sheet. Reserve the meat juices in the pan.

5 Coarsely grate the potatoes into a large bowl. Using a fork, gently stir in the chopped rosemary and season to taste. Add enough beaten egg to moisten the mixture, then mould gently over the lamb fillets. Brush with melted butter and bake in the oven for about 45 minutes or until the lamb

is cooked through and the coating is crisp and golden.

6 Meanwhile, to make the sauce, blend the cornflour with the orange juice and stir into the meat juices in the frying pan. Add the stock and sugar and bring to the boil, stirring. Add the watercress, season to taste and simmer for 1 minute or until the sauce has thickened.

7 Pour the hot sauce on to a warmed serving plate and place the lamb fillets on top. Garnish with rosemary leaves and orange slices and serve with steamed courgette and carrot ribbons and celery cooked with chestnuts.

Cherry Almond Brûlées

Morgan Jones

7 oz (200 g) canned stoned black cherries, drained

3½ oz (90 g) cream cheese, softened

2½ oz (65 g) soured cream

few drops of vanilla essence

1 oz (25 g) flaked almonds

2 oz (50 g) demerara sugar

frosted cocktail cherries, seedless grapes and mint leaves, to decorate (see page 90)

1 Divide the cherries between two individual flameproof ramekin dishes.

2 Combine the cream cheese, soured cream and vanilla essence and spoon over the cherries. Chill thoroughly in the fridge.

3 Preheat the grill to high. Sprinkle the flaked almonds over the cream cheese mixture and cover with an even layer of sugar, making sure the sugar goes right to the edges of the dishes.

4 Place under the grill for about 2 minutes or until the sugar browns and caramelises, turning the dishes occasionally if necessary.

5 Leave to cool completely, then chill in the fridge until the sugar hardens and the cream is very cold. Decorate with frosted cocktail cherries, grapes and mint leaves just before serving.

'I have chosen Franco Taruschio as my special guest. He has a happy, smiling personality and I like the way he presents his food. I have chosen Welsh lamb, butter and cream for my dishes as Franco's restaurant is in Wales, near Abergavenny, and I think he likes using local produce in his dishes as much as possible.'

Piedmontese Peppers

Franco Taruschio

1 red pepper, halved lengthways and de-seeded

1 green pepper, halved lengthways and de-seeded

4 plum tomatoes, skinned

4 anchovy fillets

1 garlic clove, finely chopped

virgin olive oil

freshly ground pepper, to taste

1 Preheat the oven to Gas Mark 5/190°C/375°F.

2 Put the pepper halves in a baking dish and place a plum tomato in each one. Top with an anchovy fillet.

3 Scatter the chopped garlic over the peppers and tomatoes and season to taste with pepper. Sprinkle liberally with olive oil.

4 Cover the dish and cook in the oven for about 20 minutes or until the peppers are *al dente*, that is tender but still slightly crisp. Serve hot or cold, accompanied by plenty of Italian bread (such as *ciabatta*).

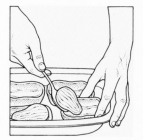

Morgan Jones, aged 11, comes from Penllergaer, Swansea, and attends the Gorseinon Junior School. Morgan's cookery skills have been learned from his mother. He also enjoys badminton and rugby as well as playing the piano and the violin. Morgan is hoping to be a pilot.

Franco Taruschio is the chef/proprietor of The Walnut Tree Inn, Abergavenny. He was born in Italy and trained at the Hotel School in Como before continuing his career in Switzerland and France. Subsequently, he came to England to work at the Three Horseshoes Hotel in Rugby.

Franco bought The Walnut Tree in 1963 and received a Gold Medal for Services to Tourism in Wales in 1985. The restaurant was awarded the Egon Ronay Restaurant of the Year Award in 1987.

Franco has appeared in a number of television programmes, including Channel 4's Take Six More Cooks in 1988, and the BBC's Masterchef in 1990.

Mozzarella Meatballs

Miranda Shearer (9) from Bridgwater

8 oz (250 g) lean organic
minced beef

1 small onion, finely chopped

1 teaspoon chopped fresh
thyme

1 tablespoon chopped fresh
parsley

1 egg, beaten

½ Mozzarella cheese
(preferably *Mozzarella di
Bufala*, made from water
buffalo's milk)

wholemeal flour, for coating

3 tablespoons olive oil

pepper, to taste

For the Sauce

1 tablespoon olive oil

½ onion, finely chopped

1 garlic clove, crushed

1 celery stick, finely chopped

5 tomatoes, skinned,
de-seeded and chopped

1 teaspoon tomato purée

1 teaspoon molasses sugar

pepper, to taste

1 To make the meatballs, put the beef, onion, herbs and beaten egg in a bowl and mix well, adding pepper to taste.

2 Cut the Mozzarella into four ¾ inch (2 cm) cubes and mould the meat mixture around each one. Roll the meatballs in flour to coat.

3 Heat the olive oil in a frying pan and fry the meatballs for 12–13 minutes or until cooked through and browned.

4 To make the sauce, heat the olive oil in a saucepan. Add the onion, garlic and celery and cook gently for about 6 minutes or until soft. Add the remaining ingredients, with pepper to taste, and continue cooking gently until the sauce is pulpy.

5 Serve the meatballs on top of boiled spaghetti sprinkled with Parmesan cheese, with the hot sauce spooned over the top.

Bishop's Delight (Flapjack and Carob Cheesecake)

Eryl Morgan (12) from Hengoed, Mid Glamorgan

Serves Four

For the Base

3 oz (75 g) margarine

2 oz (50 g) soft brown sugar

1 tablespoon golden syrup

5 oz (150 g) porridge oats

1 tablespoon carob powder

For the Filling

12 oz (375 g) low fat soft cheese

2 tablespoons natural yogurt

2 tablespoons soft brown sugar

2 eggs, separated

2 oz (50 g) carob chips

To Finish

2½ fl oz (65 ml) whipping cream

leaves made from melted carob chips

1 Preheat the oven to Gas Mark 6/200°C/400°F. Grease an 8 inch (20 cm) loose-bottomed cake tin.

2 Put the margarine, sugar and syrup in a saucepan and heat gently, stirring, until melted. Remove from the heat, add the oats and carob powder and stir until well mixed. Turn into the prepared tin and press evenly into the base. Bake in the oven for 5–10 minutes or until golden, then leave to cool. Lower the oven temperature to Gas Mark 3/160°C/325°F.

3 Blend together the cheese, yogurt, brown sugar and egg yolks. Stir in the carob chips and mix well. Whisk the egg whites until stiff and fold into the mixture. Spoon over the flapjack base and bake in the oven for about 45 minutes or until the topping is set and golden. Leave to cool in the tin.

4 Transfer the cheesecake to a serving plate and chill in the fridge. To serve, whip the cream until thick and pipe in rosettes around the top edge of the cheesecake. Scatter carob leaves over the top.

Hot Dorset Apple Cake

Jonathan Hare (13) from Taunton

Serves Four

8 oz (250 g) cooking apples

4 oz (125 g) granulated sugar

juice of ½ lemon

8 oz (250 g) self-raising flour

4 oz (125 g) margarine

1 egg, beaten

¼ teaspoon ground cinnamon

1 tablespoon demerara sugar

1 Preheat the oven to Gas Mark 4/180°C/350°F. Grease and line an 8 inch (20 cm) round cake tin with greased greaseproof paper.

2 Peel, core and finely slice the apples into a bowl. Sprinkle with the granulated sugar and lemon juice, cover and leave for 30 minutes.

3 Sift the flour into a bowl and rub in the margarine until the mixture resembles fine bread-crumbs. Fold in the beaten egg, the cinnamon and apples and mix well.

4 Turn the mixture into the prepared tin and sprinkle with demerara sugar. Bake in the oven for 20–30 minutes or until risen and springy to the touch. Turn out on to a warmed serving plate, remove the greaseproof paper and serve hot with ice cream.

Caribbean 'Eggs'

Rhian Francis (15) from Swansea

3 oz (75 g) sesame seeds

2 oz (50 g) sunflower seeds

2 oz (50 g) mixed nuts (eg. peanuts, hazelnuts, almonds and brazil nuts)

4 oz (125 g) mixed ready to eat dried fruit (eg. apricots, peaches, pineapple and bananas), roughly chopped

1½ tablespoons desiccated coconut

1 tablespoon honey

1 tablespoon orange juice

sesame seeds, to coat

1 Put the sesame seeds in a food processor with the sunflower seeds and nuts and grind well.

2 Add the dried fruit and process with the nuts and seeds until well combined. Add the coconut, honey and orange juice and process again until the mixture forms a sticky mass.

3 Remove spoonfuls of the mixture from the processor and roll into small balls about the size of eggs. Roll in sesame seeds until thoroughly coated, then chill in the fridge until ready to serve.

Banana and Walnut Crumble

Andrew Edmunds (15) from Bristol

2 oz (50 g) plain wholemeal flour

2 oz (50 g) margarine

2 oz (50 g) porridge oats

2 oz (50 g) brown sugar

2 bananas

1 oz (25 g) chopped walnuts

2 tablespoons butterscotch sauce

1 Preheat the oven to Gas Mark 6/200°C/400°F.

2 Put the flour in a bowl and rub in the margarine until the mixture resembles breadcrumbs. Stir in the oats and sugar.

3 Peel and slice the bananas into an ovenproof dish. Add the walnuts and butterscotch sauce. Cover with crumble topping and bake in the oven for 20 minutes. Serve with natural yogurt.

Smoked Trout Soufflé

This soufflé starter was suggested by popular television cook, Keith Floyd, as a suitable dish to complete Andrew Edmunds' menu (see recipe above). Andrew thought Floyd would enjoy the variations of colour and shape in his meal.

Serves Six

3 oz (75 g) butter

2 oz (50 g) plain flour

½ pint (300 ml) milk

5 eggs, separated, plus 1 more egg white

4 oz (125 g) smoked trout fillets, mashed to a thick purée with double cream

pinch of chopped fresh thyme

pinch of grated nutmeg

salt and pepper, to taste

1 Preheat the oven to Gas Mark 6/200°C/400°F. Grease a large (2½ pint/1.5 litre) soufflé dish.

2 Melt the butter in a saucepan, blend in the flour and cook for 1–2 minutes, stirring. Remove from the heat and gradually stir in the milk. Bring to the boil and cook until the sauce is thick and smooth, stirring constantly. Remove from the heat and leave to cool.

3 When the sauce is cool, stir in the egg yolks and fish purée. Season to taste and add the thyme and nutmeg.

4 Whisk all the egg whites together until stiff and fold into the fish mixture. Pour into the prepared soufflé dish and cook in the oven for 20–25 minutes or until well risen and golden. Do not open the oven door during cooking. Serve immediately.

Italian Antipasto

**For an Italian meal, this recipe from Sophie Grigson makes an ideal starter.
Try serving it before Miranda Shearer's Mozzarella Meatballs (page 42).**

4 oz (125 g) black olives

4 oz (125 g) Italian salami or
prosciutto di Parma (Parma
ham)

For the Salad

1 green pepper, quartered and
de-seeded

1 red pepper, quartered and
de-seeded

1 small garlic clove, crushed

2 tablespoons olive oil

5 canned anchovy fillets,
halved lengthways

½ tablespoon finely chopped
fresh parsley

salt and pepper, to taste

1 Preheat the grill to high.

2 To make the salad, lay the pepper pieces, skin side up, on the grill and cook until the skin is blackened and blistered all over. Drop into a polythene bag, seal and leave until cool enough to handle.

3 Remove the blackened skin and cut the peppers into thin strips. Place in a shallow serving dish and add the garlic, a little salt, plenty of pepper and the oil. Toss to mix, then arrange the anchovy fillets on top and sprinkle with chopped parsley.

4 Put the olives in a bowl and arrange the salami or *prosciutto* on a plate. Serve at room temperature with the salad and lots of fresh crusty bread.

North-East England
Winning Recipes by Jenny Docherty

Guest Cook Raymond Blanc

Courgettes en Fleur Farcies au
Coulis de Tomates Crues
(page 52)

Magrets de Canard
Sauce Pamplemousse
(page 50)

Pâte Sucrée aux
Fruits d'Été
(page 51)

Magret de Canard Sauce Pamplemousse

Jenny Docherty

2 small or 1 large boned duck breast (*magret*)

salt and pepper, to taste

For the Fillo Parcels

1 carrot, peeled and cut into small matchsticks

1 courgette, peeled

salt

3 sheets fillo pastry, thawed if frozen

1½ oz (40 g) butter, melted

1 spring onion, chopped (green tops reserved)

For the Sauce

1 tablespoon caster sugar

¼ pint (150 ml) duck stock

2 fl oz (50 ml) grapefruit juice

2 fl oz (50 ml) orange juice

½ oz (15 g) butter

To Garnish

pared rind of 1 orange

orange and grapefruit slices

1 Preheat the oven to Gas Mark 7/220°C/425°F.

2 Put the duck breast(s) in a roasting tin, season and roast in the oven for about 25 minutes.

3 Meanwhile, blanch the carrot in boiling water for 1 minute, then drain. Grate the courgette into a sieve and sprinkle with salt. Put over a bowl and chill in the fridge. Squeeze all the excess liquid out of the courgette by pressing with the back of a spoon.

4 To make the sauce, put the sugar in a heavy-based saucepan with 2 teaspoons water and heat gently until it melts and turns brown. Remove from the heat and carefully add the duck stock and fruit juices. Bring to the boil and boil rapidly until reduced by half, then beat in the butter to thicken.

5 To assemble the fillo parcels, brush the sheets of fillo with melted butter and pile one on top of the other. Cut into two squares and put half the carrot, courgette and chopped spring onion in the centre of each.

6 Draw the fillo pastry up round the vegetables and form into 'pouch' shapes. Tie the necks with strips of spring onion tops. Place on a baking sheet, brush with more melted butter and bake in the oven for 8–10 minutes.

7 Meanwhile, for the garnish, cut the orange rind into julienne strips and blanch in boiling water for 2 minutes. Drain, and refresh in cold water.

8 To serve, drain the fat from the duck and cut into slices. Arrange on a serving plate with the sauce and garnish with orange and grapefruit slices and strips of orange rind. Serve with the fillo parcels and a warm salad of mixed leaves and lightly fried oyster mushrooms dressed with a balsamic vinegar dressing.

Pâte Sucrée aux Fruits d'Été

Jenny Docherty

For the Pastry

4½ oz (140 g) plain flour

3½ oz (90 g) butter, diced

1¾ oz (45 g) icing sugar

pinch of salt

1 egg yolk

1 drop vanilla essence

For the Filling and Coulis

4 oz (125 g) raspberries

icing sugar, to taste

lemon juice, to taste

4 oz (125 g) strawberries, hulled

To Decorate

strawberries

raspberries

strawberry leaves and flowers (optional)

1 Preheat the oven to Gas Mark 6/200°C/400°F.

2 To make the pastry, sift the flour on to a work surface or board and make a well in the centre. Add the butter and work with your fingertips until soft.

3 Sift the icing sugar on to the butter, add the salt and work in. Add the egg yolk and mix well, then gradually draw in the flour, working with your fingertips until thoroughly combined. Add the vanilla and knead in lightly.

4 Divide the pastry into two equal pieces and roll out on a lightly floured surface to a thickness of about ⅛ inch (3 mm). Cut three circles from each piece of pastry using a 4 inch (10 cm) fluted cutter. Place on a baking sheet and bake in the oven for 8 minutes or until pale golden. Leave to cool.

5 To make the coulis, put the raspberries in a saucepan with icing sugar to taste and a little water and heat gently, mashing the raspberries with a wooden spoon. Cool slightly, then pass through a nylon sieve. Add a little lemon juice to taste.

6 To assemble, place a pastry circle in the centre of each of two serving plates. Slice the strawberries, dip in the coulis and arrange a few on each pastry base. Cover with another pastry round and repeat the layers of strawberries and pastry, ending with a round of pastry. Sprinkle with a little icing sugar and decorate with wedges of strawberry, raspberries and strawberry flowers and leaves, if available.

7 To serve, pour a thin ribbon of raspberry coulis around the pastries.

'I think Raymond Blanc would like to eat my meal for the following reasons: Firstly, from reading his book, I think he likes duck and I think my sauce might be to his taste. Secondly, I have adapted the fillo parcels from one of his recipes. Finally, he might like the novelty of an accompanying warm mushroom salad dressed with a balsamic vinegar dressing instead of potato or pasta.'

Courgettes en Fleur Farcies au Coulis de Tomates Crues

Raymond Blanc

4 small courgettes with their flowers

2½ pints (1.5 litres) water

1 tablespoon olive oil

small sprig fresh thyme

very small sprig fresh marjoram

salt and pepper, to taste

For the Vegetable Brunoise (Stuffing)

1 tablespoon olive oil

½ small courgette, finely diced

½ garlic clove, halved

1½ tomatoes, peeled, de-seeded and diced

2 leaves fresh basil, shredded

salt and pepper, to taste

For the Tomato Coulis

3 ripe tomatoes

¼ oz (10 g) unsalted butter, chilled and diced

1½ tablespoons olive oil

pinch of caster sugar (optional)

salt and pepper, to taste

1 To prepare the courgettes and flowers, carefully detach the flowers from the courgettes and neatly cut off the ends of the stalks. Open up the flowers and rinse out the insides with running water.

2 Bring the water to the boil, add salt to taste and the courgettes and blanch for 3 minutes, then drain, reserving the cooking water, and refresh in plenty of cold water. Drain again and place on a tray lined with kitchen paper.

3 Slide the flowers carefully into the same boiling water for 5 seconds only. Drain, gently shake out any excess water and put on the tray with the courgettes.

4 Preheat the oven to Gas Mark 8/230°C/450°F.

5 For the brunoise, heat 1 tablespoon olive oil in a frying pan and fry the diced courgette with the garlic for 2 minutes. Add the diced tomatoes and basil, season to taste with salt and pepper and cook for 1 minute.

6 Remove the garlic, then slice it finely and reserve it for the tomato coulis. Leave to cool.

7 Open up the courgette flowers, using a teaspoon, and carefully fill them with the courgette and tomato mixture, twisting the end of each flower to hold in the stuffing. Place on a large tray.

8 To make the tomato coulis, halve the tomatoes and place in a blender or food processor with the reserved garlic. Blend to a purée, then pass through a sieve into a saucepan. Warm over a low heat, without boiling, then whisk in the cold butter. Gradually whisk in the olive oil. Season to taste with salt and pepper and a little sugar, if required. Remove from the heat.

9 Cut the blanched courgettes lengthways into several slices, leaving one end intact, and fan them out. Season the courgettes and stuffed flowers to taste with a little salt and pepper.

10 In a large non-stick frying pan, heat 1 tablespoon olive oil with the thyme and marjoram. Add the courgettes and fry for 20 seconds, then turn and cook for a further 20 seconds. Add the stuffed

flowers and fry for 5 seconds on each side.

11 Place the frying pan in the oven for about 3 minutes, then remove and keep warm. Check the seasoning.

12 To serve, spoon the warm tomato coulis on to two warmed plates. Arrange the fanned courgettes in the centre and add the flowers. Sprinkle with a little pepper and serve at once.

Jenny Docherty, aged 14, lives in Broom Park, Durham and attends the Durham High School.
Jenny is taking Home Economics at school but has also been taught to cook by her parents. Her other interests include drawing, painting, reading and collecting things. Her career aspirations lie in the field of medicine or aviation; she would like to be a doctor or a pilot.

Raymond Blanc is chef and proprietor of the world-famous restaurant and hotel, Le Manoir aux Quat' Saisons at Great Milton, Oxford. Raymond began his career working as a waiter in a restaurant and in 1972 came to England as a head chef. He opened his first restaurant in 1977, followed by Le Manoir in 1984. Le Manoir is one of only nine hotels in the world to hold the Relais & Château Gold and Red Shields, and has been the recipient of numerous other top awards.

As well as publishing his own book of recipes, *Le Manoir aux Quat' Saisons*, Raymond has contributed to a number of other publications and has made several television appearances, including on the BBC's Food and Drink and Channel 4's Take Six Cooks.

Baked Turbot with Wild Mushrooms and Mussel Sauce

David Graham (15) from Chester Le Street

2 turbot steaks

1 onion, finely sliced

½ pint (300 ml) fish stock

10 mussels, scrubbed and soaked

½ pint (300 ml) single cream

5 oz (150 g) butter

4 oz (125 g) mixed wild mushrooms (eg. oyster, shiitake or pleurotte), trimmed and cleaned

salt and pepper, to taste

sprigs fresh chervil, to garnish

1 Preheat the oven to Gas Mark 6/200°C/400°F.

2 Put the turbot in a buttered ovenproof dish with the onion and fish stock. Season to taste, cover and bake in the oven for 10 minutes.

3 Meanwhile, bring a little water to the boil in a large saucepan, add the mussels, cover tightly and cook for about 5 minutes or until the mussels are cooked and the shells have opened. Drain the mussels, discard any that have not opened, and remove the remainder from their shells.

4 When the fish is cooked, strain the liquid from the dish into a saucepan. Place the fish in a warmed serving dish and keep warm.

5 Boil the fish cooking liquid rapidly to reduce by half, then add the cream. Reduce by half again, then add 4 oz (125 g) of the butter. Add the mussels and heat through gently. Check the seasoning.

6 Meanwhile, melt the remaining butter in a saucepan and cook the mushrooms for 3–5 minutes or until soft.

7 Garnish the turbot with chervil sprigs and serve with the sauce and wild mushrooms.

Continental Lentil Toad in the Hole

Christina Sturge (13) from York

2 oz (50 g) continental (green) lentils, rinsed

2 tablespoons vegetable oil

½ onion, chopped

½ garlic clove, crushed

2 oz (50 g) mushrooms, wiped and sliced

½ teaspoon dried thyme

sea salt and freshly ground black pepper, to taste

For the Batter

2 oz (50 g) self-raising wholemeal flour

¼ teaspoon sea salt

1 egg

¼ pint (150 ml) milk

1 Cook the lentils in boiling water for 30–45 minutes or until tender. Drain well.

2 Preheat the oven to Gas Mark 7/220°C/425°F.

3 Heat 1 tablespoon of the oil in a saucepan and fry the onion and garlic for 5 minutes or until slightly browned. Add the mushrooms and fry for another 5 minutes. Stir in the lentils and thyme and season to taste with sea salt and freshly ground black pepper. Keep the mixture hot.

4 To make the batter, sift the flour and salt into a bowl, then add any bran left in the sieve. Make a well in the centre and add the egg and one third of the milk. Beat vigorously with a wooden spoon, gradually incorporating the flour and the remaining milk. Beat well.

5 Put the remaining oil in a shallow baking tin and heat in the oven. Pour the batter straight into the hot oil, then quickly spoon the lentil mixture on top. Bake in the oven for 20–25 minutes or until risen and golden. Serve with lightly boiled or steamed broccoli and carrots.

Porcini Risotto

Sophia Winfield (10) from York

½ oz (15 g) dried porcini (cep) mushrooms

¼ pint (150 ml) hot water

1 pint (600 ml) chicken stock

2 tablespoons olive oil

2 shallots, finely chopped

5 oz (150 g) Arborio or risotto rice

3 fl oz (75 ml) dry white wine

2 oz (50 g) shiitake mushrooms, trimmed, cleaned and sliced

2 oz (50 g) oyster mushrooms, trimmed, cleaned and sliced

1 oz (25 g) butter

2 tablespoons chopped fresh parsley

salt and pepper, to taste

freshly grated Parmesan cheese, to serve

1 Soak the porcini mushrooms in the hot water for at least 30 minutes. Drain, reserving the soaking water.

2 Put the stock in a saucepan, add the porcini soaking water, bring just to the boil and keep hot.

3 Heat the olive oil in a heavy-based saucepan and fry the shallots for 3–5 minutes or until soft. Add the rice and stir to coat in the oil. Cook, stirring, until the rice is transparent.

4 Add the wine to the rice and let it bubble for 1 minute, then add the shiitake,

oyster and porcini mushrooms with a ladleful of hot stock. Continue cooking over a medium heat for about 20 minutes, adding more stock as it is needed.

5 Remove the risotto from the heat and stir in the butter and parsley. Season to taste with salt and pepper. Spoon on to warmed serving plates and serve at once, accompanied by Parmesan cheese.

Once-brewed Chocolate Supremes

David Macdonald (15) from Bardon Mill

2 oz (50 g) plain chocolate

2 eggs, separated

1¾ oz (45 g) butter, diced (at room temperature)

½ tablespoon Tia Maria

2 teaspoons icing sugar, sifted

1½ tablespoons double cream

To Decorate

½ oz (15 g) chopped nuts

1 oz (25 g) plain chocolate, grated

1 Break up the chocolate and put it in a small microwave-proof bowl. Microwave on HIGH (100%) for 2 minutes or until melted, stirring once. (Alternatively, melt the chocolate in a heatproof bowl over a saucepan of gently simmering water.)

2 Add the egg yolks to the melted chocolate and mix gently; do not beat. Add the butter and stir gently until melted. Add the Tia Maria and icing sugar and stir until dissolved. Add the cream and stir again.

3 Whisk the egg whites until thick and fluffy and fold into the chocolate mixture. Divide between two serving glasses, cover and chill in the fridge until required. Serve decorated with nuts and grated chocolate.

Crêpes Soufflé avec Coulis de Framboise

Graham Campbell (14) from Ponteland

For the Crêpes

4 oz (125 g) plain flour

2 eggs

¼ pint (150 ml) milk

3 fl oz (75 ml) water

1 oz (25 g) butter

For the Filling

1 egg white

1 tablespoon caster sugar

2 teaspoons lemon juice

1 firm kiwi fruit, peeled and thinly sliced

For the Coulis

5 oz (150 g) raspberries

2 oz (50 g) caster sugar

juice of ¼ lemon

1 Preheat the oven to Gas Mark 5/190°C/375°F.

2 To make the crêpes, put the flour, eggs, milk and water in a food processor and blend to a smooth batter.

3 Heat a small crêpe pan, then add a little butter, tilting the pan so that the butter coats the base and slightly up the sides of the pan as it melts. Pour off any excess.

4 Pour in enough batter to coat the base of the pan thinly and cook for 1–2 minutes or until set and golden brown underneath. Toss the crêpe (or turn with a spatula) and cook the second side until golden. Slide the crêpe on to a plate and leave to cool. Make a second crêpe in the same way.

5 For the filling, whisk the egg white until stiff, then fold in the sugar and lemon juice. Spread a good tablespoonful of filling on one half of each crêpe and top with slices of kiwi fruit. Fold over the crêpes and place on a well buttered baking sheet. Heat in the oven for 5 minutes.

6 Meanwhile, to make the coulis, put the raspberries and sugar in a food processor and blend for 30 seconds. Add the lemon juice, then pass through muslin or a nylon sieve.

7 To serve, place each crêpe on a warmed serving plate and surround with the coulis.

Watercress Soup

As a well known writer on vegetarian cookery, Rose Elliot provided this recipe as a good starter to serve before Christina Sturge's Continental Lentil Toad in the Hole (page 55). Christina chose to cook for Rose Elliott because she is a vegetarian herself.

Serves Four

1 bunch watercress

2 pints (1.2 litres) water

1 lb (500 g) potatoes, diced

1 onion, chopped

4 tablespoons single cream

freshly grated nutmeg, to taste

salt and pepper, to taste

1 Separate the leaves from the watercress stalks. Reserve the leaves and put the stalks in a large saucepan with the water, potatoes and onion. Bring to the boil, then simmer for 15–20 minutes or until the vegetables are tender. Leave to cool slightly.

2 Pour the soup into an electric blender or food processor. Add the reserved watercress leaves and blend until smooth. Add the cream and season to taste with nutmeg, salt and pepper. If serving hot, reheat gently, without boiling.

Gamberoni in Camicia (Prawns in Pastry Cases)

This Italian starter was created by Antonio Carluccio of the Neal Street Restaurant in London's Covent Garden. Antonio is well known for his passion for mushrooms – one reason why Sophia Winfield chose to cook Porcini Risotto (page 56) for him.

Serves Four

3 oz (75 g) puff pastry, thawed if frozen

1 egg, beaten

1 tablespoon finely chopped fresh parsley

1 teaspoon chopped fresh dill

2 oz (50 g) ricotta or curd cheese

8 large Dublin Bay prawns, peeled

salt and pepper, to taste

1 Preheat the oven to Gas Mark 7/220°C/425°F. Oil a baking sheet.

2 Put the pastry on a lightly floured surface and roll out as thinly as possible. Cut into eight 4 inch (10 cm) squares.

3 Remove about 1 teaspoon of the beaten egg and reserve for brushing. Add the herbs to the remaining egg, season to taste with salt and pepper, then add the ricotta or curd cheese and mix well.

4 Place one prawn diagonally on each pastry square and add a spoonful of the egg, cheese and herb mixture. Roll over and fold in the pastry points to form an 'envelope' and brush with the reserved beaten egg to seal.

5 Place the pastry cases side by side on the oiled baking sheet and bake in the oven for 15 minutes.

Scotland

Winning Recipes by Katherine Gray

Guest Cook Ferrier Richardson

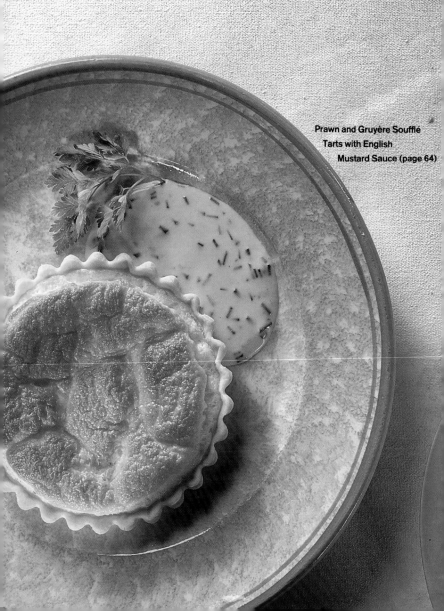

**Prawn and Gruyère Soufflé
Tarts with English
Mustard Sauce (page 64)**

Scottish Salmon with Potato Scales (page 62)

Warm Fillo Parcels of Exotic Fruit and Berries (page 63)

Scottish Salmon with Potato Scales

Katherine Gray

2 tablespoons olive oil

two 6 oz (175 g) salmon fillets
(preferably wild)

2 large potatoes

melted butter, for brushing

1 carrot

¼ turnip

1 courgette

2 fl oz (50 ml) dry white wine

2 fl oz (50 ml) fish stock

4 oz (125 g) butter, chilled and
diced

¼ pint (142 ml) carton double
cream

1 tablespoon snipped chives

salt and pepper, to taste

fresh chervil sprigs, to garnish
(optional)

1 Preheat the oven to Gas Mark 8/230°C/450°F. Place a piece of greaseproof paper on a baking sheet and brush with olive oil.

2 Season the salmon with salt and pepper and place on the lined baking sheet.

3 Peel the potatoes, slice very thinly and cut into neat rounds. Brush with melted butter and arrange over the salmon, overlapping, to represent fish scales. Season with salt and pepper to taste and bake in the oven for 8 minutes.

4 Meanwhile, prepare the vegetables with a solterino cutter (small melon baller), blanch for 2–3 minutes, then drain, refresh in cold water and drain again.

5 Put the white wine and fish stock in a saucepan and bring to the boil. Remove the pan to the edge of the hob and add the butter, one piece at a time, stirring until each piece has melted. Stir in the cream, add the vegetables and check the seasoning.

6 Place the salmon in the centre of a warmed serving plate. Add the chives to the sauce and pour round the salmon.

7 Garnish with fresh chervil (if using) and serve with steamed asparagus.

Warm Fillo Parcels of Exotic Fruit and Berries

Katherine Gray

¼ pint (142 ml) carton single cream

¼ vanilla pod

2 egg yolks (size 2)

1 oz (25 g) caster sugar

2 sheets fillo pastry, thawed if frozen

2 oz (50 g) butter, melted

8 oz (250 g) mixed exotic fruits and berries (eg. redcurrants, blueberries, star fruit and kiwi fruit), chopped or sliced if necessary

1 oz (25 g) flaked almonds

4 oz (125 g) raspberries

icing sugar, to taste

To Decorate

2 sprigs fresh mint

2 physalis (Cape gooseberries) or redcurrants

1 Preheat the oven to Gas Mark 6/200°C/400°F.

2 Put the cream and vanilla pod in a small saucepan, bring to just below boiling point, then remove from the heat and leave to infuse for about 10 minutes.

3 Beat the egg yolks and sugar together in a heat-proof bowl and strain in the warm cream. Discard the vanilla pod. Stand the bowl over a pan of simmering water and cook gently, stirring constantly with a wooden spoon, until the sauce is thick enough to coat the back of the spoon. Leave to cool.

4 Cut the fillo sheets in half widthways. Brush two pieces with melted butter and place one on top of the other. Pile half the mixed fruit in the centre, draw up the pastry around it and mould into a 'money pouch' shape. Repeat to make a second fillo parcel.

5 Brush the parcels with more butter, place on a baking sheet and sprinkle with the flaked almonds. Bake in the oven for 8–10 minutes or until crisp.

6 Meanwhile, put the raspberries in a food processor with a little icing sugar to taste and blend to a purée, then sieve.

7 To serve, spread the vanilla sauce on two serving plates and sprinkle with drops of raspberry coulis. Draw the point of a cocktail stick through the sauce to create a 'feathered' effect. Dust the fillo parcels with icing sugar, then place in the centre of the sauce. Decorate with mint and physalis or redcurrants.

'My chosen chef, Ferrier Richardson, owns Restaurant October and October Café. I think he would like to eat my meal because he was executive chef at the Rogano Restaurant, which is famous for its fish dishes. He also likes contrasting flavours in food and different temperatures – either hot or cold or hot with cold. The special tempting ingredient in my menu is wild Scottish salmon.'

Prawn and Gruyère Soufflé Tarts with English Mustard Sauce

Ferrier Richardson

2 oz (50 g) shortcrust pastry, thawed if frozen

2 egg whites (size 5)

small pinch of salt

1½ oz (40 g) Gruyère cheese, grated

2 oz (50 g) peeled prawns

2 sprigs fresh chervil, to garnish

For the Béchamel Sauce

7 fl oz (200 ml) milk

small piece of onion

½ carrot, sliced

⅓ celery stick, chopped

small bay leaf

2 black peppercorns

¾ oz (20 g) butter

¾ oz (20 g) plain flour

1 egg yolk

salt and pepper, to taste

For the Mustard Sauce

1 tablespoon white wine

¼ pint (142 ml) carton double cream

½ tablespoon prepared English mustard

½ tablespoon finely chopped fresh chives

salt and pepper, to taste

1 Preheat the oven to Gas Mark 6/200°C/400°F.

2 Roll out the pastry and use to line two 3½ inch (9 cm) diameter, 1 inch (2.5 cm) deep loose-bottomed tartlet tins. Line with greaseproof paper or foil and bake blind in the oven for about 10 minutes or until golden. Remove from the oven and remove the paper or foil but leave the pastry in the tins.

3 To make the béchamel sauce, put the milk in a saucepan with the vegetables and flavourings and bring slowly to the boil. Remove from the heat and leave to infuse for 30 minutes, then strain, reserving the milk.

4 Melt the butter in another saucepan, stir in the flour and cook for 1 minute, stirring. Remove from the heat and gradually blend in the flavoured milk. Bring to the boil and continue to cook, stirring, until the sauce is smooth and thick. Simmer gently for 3 minutes, then remove from the heat, season to taste with salt and pepper and beat in the egg yolk.

5 Put the egg whites in a clean bowl with the salt and whisk until stiff. Gently fold in the béchamel sauce, then the Gruyère cheese, and finally the prawns.

6 Spoon the mixture into the pastry cases and bake in the oven until the soufflés have risen and are golden brown.

7 Meanwhile, to make the mustard sauce, put the white wine in a saucepan and boil rapidly until reduced by half. Add the double cream and cook, stirring with a wooden spoon, until the sauce is thick enough to coat the back of the spoon. Whisk in the mustard and salt and pepper to taste, then stir in the chives.

8 To serve, lift the tarts out of the tins and place on warmed serving plates. Surround with mustard sauce and garnish with chervil.

Katherine Gray, aged 14, lives in Bearsden, Glasgow, and she attends the Laurel Bank School, Hillhead.

Katherine's skills in the kitchen were acquired at her Home Economics classes at school. Her hobbies include karate, tennis, reading and sketching and she is hoping to continue her education at university or college.

Ferrier Richardson is proprietor of Restaurant October in Glasgow and has gained a considerable reputation for his creativity and individual approach to cooking. His personal philosophy as far as cooking is concerned is 'the elimination of all pretentious ingredients and the use of fresh seasonal produce'.

Among his many accolades, Ferrier Richardson was Scottish Master Chef in 1989 and represented his country winning a medal at the World Culinary Olympics in Frankfurt, Germany, in 1988.

Lemon Chicken

Michael Guest (10) from Edinburgh

2 chicken breast fillets, skinned

grated rind and juice of 2 lemons

1 tablespoon plain flour

½ teaspoon paprika

2 tablespoons sunflower oil

3 fl oz (75 ml) chicken stock

2 tablespoons soft brown sugar

salt and pepper, to taste

1 Preheat the oven to Gas Mark 4/180°C/350°F.

2 Put the chicken in a bowl with the lemon juice, cover and leave to marinate in the fridge for about 15 minutes.

3 Put the flour, paprika and salt and pepper to taste in a polythene bag. Remove the chicken from the lemon juice and reserve the lemon juice. Dry the chicken with kitchen paper and place in the polythene bag. Seal and shake well until the chicken pieces are thoroughly coated.

4 Heat the oil in a frying pan and fry the chicken for 5 minutes on each side or until evenly browned. Remove from the pan and place in a casserole.

5 Mix the stock with the reserved lemon juice marinade and pour over the chicken. Sprinkle over the brown sugar and grated lemon rind and bake in the oven for 25 minutes.

6 Serve the chicken with boiled new potatoes and sugar snap peas.

Scotland

Sole Véronique with Shrimp Sauce

Gordon Innes (12) from Blairmore by Dunoon

2 sole fillets

4 tablespoons white wine

1 oz (25 g) butter

1 oz (25 g) plain flour

½ pint (300 ml) milk

4 oz (125 g) peeled, cooked shrimps, thawed if frozen

4 oz (125 g) seedless green grapes, peeled

salt and pepper, to taste

fennel leaves, to garnish

1 Roll up the fish fillets and place in a small saucepan. Pour over the wine and add salt and pepper to taste. Cover and poach for about 10 minutes.

2 Meanwhile, to make the sauce, melt the butter in a saucepan, stir in the flour and cook for 1–2 minutes. Remove from the heat and gradually blend in the milk. Bring slowly to the boil, stirring all the time until the sauce is smooth and creamy. Stir in the shrimps and grapes.

3 Remove the fish from the pan and place in a warmed serving dish. Pour over the sauce, garnish with fennel and serve at once, accompanied by lightly boiled or steamed asparagus.

Ellen's Peaches

Ellen Mathieson (13) from Pitlochry

2 large ripe peaches

1 oz (25 g) whole blanched almonds

1 fl oz (25 ml) Cognac

1 fl oz (25 ml) peach liqueur

2½ fl oz (65 ml) double cream

To Decorate

2 chocolate leaves

12 small silver dragees

1 Put the peaches in a bowl, cover with boiling water and leave to stand for 1–2 minutes. Drain, immerse in cold water, then peel off the skins.

2 Cut the almonds into thin strips and stud each peach with the strips. Stand the peaches in a shallow dish and spoon over the Cognac and liqueur. Cover and chill in the fridge for 30 minutes.

3 Spoon a pool of cream on to each of two dessert plates and place a peach in the centre of each one. Decorate each with a chocolate leaf. Spoon a little of the Cognac and liqueur marinade over the peaches, then scatter six dragees over each one.

Atholl Brose Creams

Callum Lawson (13) from Skene, Aberdeenshire

2 tablespoons medium oatmeal

6 fl oz (175 ml) double cream

about 1 tablespoon clear heather honey

about 1 tablespoon whisky

1 Put the oatmeal in a small heavy-based saucepan and heat gently, stirring, until golden. Leave to cool.

2 Whip the cream until it forms soft peaks, then whip in 1 tablespoon each of the honey and whisky. Stir in 1 tablespoon toasted oatmeal, taste the cream and add more honey or whisky if needed. Spoon into two serving glasses and chill in the fridge until required.

3 Sprinkle the tops of the creams with the remaining toasted oatmeal and serve with fresh raspberries or grapes.

Cinnamon-topped Bread and Butter Pudding

Melody Cox (13) from Bridge of Weir, Renfrewshire

4 slices white bread, crusts removed

1½ oz (40 g) butter, softened

2 oz (50 g) sultanas

1½ oz (40 g) caster sugar

1½ teaspoons ground cinnamon

2 eggs

¾ pint (450 ml) milk

1½ tablespoons granulated sugar

1 Preheat the oven to Gas Mark 3/160°C/325°F. Butter a 2 pint (1.2 litre) ovenproof dish.

2 Spread the bread slices with butter and cut into fingers or small squares.

3 Put half the bread in the prepared dish and sprinkle with the sultanas and half the caster sugar. Cover with the remaining bread, buttered side up, and sprinkle with the remaining sugar and the cinnamon.

4 Beat the eggs and milk together and strain into the dish over the bread. Sprinkle with the granulated sugar. Leave to stand for 30 minutes, then bake in the oven for 45–60 minutes or until the pudding is set and the top crisp and golden.

Ham and Fresh Figs

This classic but simple starter was suggested by well known television cook Keith Floyd. Callum Lawson decided to create his meal for Keith Floyd because he wanted to give him a taste of Scotland. Callum's Atholl Brose Creams (page 68) are based on an old traditional Scottish dish.

Serves Four

16 very ripe fresh figs, chilled overnight

14 oz (425 g) *Prosciutto di Parma* (Parma ham), very thinly sliced

1 Cut the figs into four wedges from top to bottom, but without cutting right through.

2 Open out the figs and arrange on a serving platter with the ham slices.

Steamed Spare Ribs with Black Beans

Ken Hom is well known as a food consultant and teacher and has made numerous television appearances and radio broadcasts. This Chinese starter can be made ahead, then reheated by steaming for 20 minutes or until the ribs are hot.

Serves Two to Four

1½ lb (750 g) pork spare ribs, cut into individual ribs

1 teaspoon salt

4 fl oz (125 ml) chicken stock

1 tablespoon light soy sauce

1 teaspoon sesame oil

1 teaspoon finely chopped fresh root ginger

1½ tablespoons coarsely chopped black beans

2 teaspoons finely chopped garlic

½ teaspoon salt

1 teaspoon sugar

1 tablespoon dry sherry or rice wine

1 Cut the spare ribs into 2 inch (5 cm) pieces and rub with salt. Put in a bowl and set aside for 20–25 minutes.

2 Bring a large saucepan of water to the boil, then add the spare ribs, simmer for 10 minutes, then drain.

3 Mix the remaining ingredients in a large bowl and add the spare ribs, turning to coat well with the mixture. Transfer to a deep heatproof plate or dish.

4 Set up a steamer or put a rack into a wok or large, deep saucepan. Pour in 2 inches (5 cm) water and bring to the boil. Reduce the heat, then lower the plate of spare ribs carefully into the steamer or on to the rack. Cover with a lid and steam gently for 1 hour or until the spare ribs are very tender, adding more water as necessary. Skim off any surface fat and serve.

North-West England
Winning Recipes by Amy Gibson

Guest Cook John Tovey

**Spiced Herdwick Lamb
(page 74)**

Miller Howe
Mushroom Pâté
(page 76)

Rich Chocolate
Mousses with
Cointreau (page 75)

Spiced Herdwick Lamb

Amy Gibson

3 tablespoons rosemary jelly

1 garlic clove, crushed

1 inch (2.5 cm) piece fresh root ginger, peeled and grated

½ teaspoon chilli powder

pinch of mixed dried herbs

2 lamb chops

1 tablespoon vegetable oil

salt and pepper, to taste

sprigs fresh rosemary, to garnish

1 Preheat the oven to Gas Mark 6/200°C/400°F. Grease a small, shallow casserole.

2 Mix together the jelly, garlic, ginger, chilli and herbs and spread over the chops.

3 Put the oil in the prepared casserole and add the chops. Season to taste with salt and pepper, cover with foil and cook in the oven for about 30 minutes or until the chops are tender.

4 Serve the chops straight from the casserole, accompanied by baked jacket potatoes, mange tout and carrots cooked in Vermouth. Garnish with rosemary.

Rich Chocolate Mousses with Cointreau

Amy Gibson

4 oz (125 g) plain dessert chocolate

2 eggs, separated

1 tablespoon Cointreau

To Decorate

2 heaped teaspoons whipped cream

grated chocolate or chopped toasted nuts

1 Break up the chocolate and put it in a heatproof bowl over a pan of simmering water. Heat gently, stirring, until melted, then remove from the heat.

2 Beat the egg yolks, add them to the chocolate while it is still hot and beat thoroughly. Leave to cool for 2 minutes.

3 Whisk the egg whites until soft peaks form and fold into the chocolate mixture. Spoon into two serving glasses, cover with foil and chill in the fridge.

4 Just before serving, make small holes in the tops of the mousses with a fine skewer and pour over the Cointreau. Leave to soak in, then decorate the mousses with whipped cream and grated chocolate or chopped toasted nuts.

'As my guest cook, I have chosen John Tovey, the well-known cook and restaurateur. He would very much like to eat my meal because he likes alcohol in food; the Vermouth and Cointreau are my special tempting ingredients. I have been told that each evening at Miller Howe, John Tovey opens a bottle of wine to share with his staff while they discuss the evening. He is also renowned for his sweet tooth and for his wickedly rich puddings, so I think this meal would be ideal.'

Miller Howe Mushroom Pâté

John Tovey

Serves Four

4 oz (125 g) butter

8 oz (250 g) onions, minced

2 lb (1 kg) mushrooms, minced

1 pint (600 ml) red wine

generous pinch of sea salt and freshly ground black pepper, to taste

1 Melt the butter in a large saucepan over a low heat. Add the onions and cook gently for about 10 minutes, then add the mushrooms, salt and pepper to taste. Stir well.

2 Add the red wine and leave to simmer, uncovered, over a very low heat, for 2–3 hours or until the liquid has evaporated and the mixture is fairly dry, stirring occasionally. Leave to cool, then pack into small ramekin dishes or serving pots and chill in the fridge until required.

3 Serve the pâté with crusty French bread, granary rolls or Melba toast.

Fourteen-year-old Amy Gibson lives in Carnforth, Lancashire, and she attends the Casterton School in Kirkby Lonsdale. Amy's mother has taught her many of her culinary skills but she also studies Home Economics at school and has attended evening classes. Her hobbies include riding, squash, tennis and swimming, and she is interested in history and languages.

John Tovey is the well-known proprietor of the Miller Howe Hotel and Restaurant overlooking Lake Windermere in the Lake District. He is an established cookery author and has had a number of books published, including the *Radio Times Cook Book, Entertaining with Tovey, Feast of Vegetables* and *The Miller Howe Cookbook*.

Dijon Kidneys

Carl Denovan (13) from Macclesfield

2 teaspoons butter

1 onion, finely chopped

9 lambs' kidneys, skinned, cored and roughly chopped

1 oz (25 g) plain flour

2 fl oz (50 ml) dry Vermouth

4 fl oz (125 ml) milk

1 tablespoon Dijon mustard

1 tablespoon Worcestershire sauce

pinch of cayenne

2 fl oz (50 ml) double or whipping cream

salt and pepper, to taste

1 Heat the butter in a frying pan and fry the onion over a moderate heat for about 3 minutes. Add the kidneys and cook over a high heat, stirring, for 5 minutes or until sealed.

2 Sprinkle the flour into the pan and continue to cook over a moderate heat for 10 minutes, stirring the flour into the kidneys.

3 Gradually add the Vermouth, milk, mustard, Worcestershire sauce and cayenne and cook for a further 5 minutes. Check the seasoning, add the cream and serve with boiled rice or noodles.

Quail Stuffed with Kibbeh

Sophie Bracewell (13) from Preston

2 oz (50 g) burghul (bulgar wheat)

2 oz (50 g) boned, trimmed and cubed leg of lamb

1 oz (25 g) onion, roughly chopped

½ teaspoon cumin seeds, roasted

½ teaspoon mixed ground cloves, cinnamon, nutmeg and pepper

4 oven-ready quails

2 tablespoons olive oil

2 teaspoons lemon juice

½ teaspoon mixed salt, ground allspice and cinnamon

1 Preheat the oven to Gas Mark 3/160°C/325°F. Put the burghul in a bowl, cover with cold water and leave to soak for 20 minutes, then drain well.

2 To make the kibbeh, rinse and drain the burghul and put it in a food processor. Add the lamb and onion and process to a paste.

3 Mix the cumin seeds and spice mix into the burghul mixture and spoon into the quails. Pull the end flap over the opening of each bird and put in a roasting tin. Mix the oil, lemon juice and spiced salt and use to baste the quails.

4 Cook in the oven for 10 minutes, baste again, then cook for a further 10 minutes. Serve with boiled rice and a mixed green salad.

Trout Parcels

Anna-Marie Reynolds (13) from Lytham St. Anne's

1½ tablespoons olive oil

2 trout, cleaned

½ onion, finely chopped

1 celery stick, trimmed and sliced

½ tablespoon chopped fresh parsley

½ garlic clove, crushed

½ teaspoon chopped fresh oregano or ¼ teaspoon dried

juice of ¼ lemon

salt and pepper, to taste

1 Preheat the oven to Gas Mark 5/190°C/375°F. Cut two pieces of foil, each large enough to enclose one fish, and brush with a little oil.

2 Place each fish on a piece of foil, season with salt and pepper and brush with more oil.

3 Heat 1 tablespoon olive oil in a small frying pan, add the onion and celery and fry for 10 minutes. Add the parsley, garlic, oregano and lemon juice and season with a little salt and pepper.

4 Spread the vegetable mixture over the two fish, wrap round the foil and seal. Bake in the oven for 20 minutes.

5 Serve the fish in the half-opened foil parcels with baked jacket potatoes and a salad garnish.

Luscious Lemon Pudding

Hannah Merton (12) from Warrington

1 oz (25 g) butter

2 oz (50 g) caster sugar

grated rind and juice of
1 lemon

2 eggs, separated

1 oz (25 g) self-raising flour

¼ pint (150 ml) water

1 Preheat the oven to Gas Mark 4/180°C/350°F.

2 Cream the butter and sugar together. Beat in the lemon rind and egg yolks, then stir in the flour, lemon juice and water.

3 Whisk the egg whites until stiff, then fold into the lemon mixture and pour into a greased ovenproof dish. Put the dish in a roasting tin and pour enough water into the tin to come halfway up the side of the dish. Cook the pudding near the bottom of the oven for 25 minutes.

4 During cooking, the pudding separates to form a very light sponge topping with a lemon sauce base. Serve hot.

Banana Fritters

Catherine Croyston (14) from Wilmslow

3 large bananas

1 tablespoon plain flour

1½ oz (40 g) cornflour

½ teaspoon baking powder

¼ teaspoon salt

4 fl oz (125 ml) milk

1 egg white

oil, for deep frying

2 oz (50 g) caster sugar

1 Peel the bananas and cut each one into three.

2 Sift the flour, cornflour, baking powder and salt into a bowl and gradually add the milk, mixing to a smooth batter. Whisk the egg white until soft peaks form and fold lightly into the batter.

3 Heat the oil in a deep fat fryer to 180°C (350°F).

Drop the banana pieces, one at a time, into the batter, then deep-fry until golden brown. Remove from the oil and drain on kitchen paper.

4 Toss the fritters in caster sugar before serving hot with whipped cream or ice cream.

Santa Claus'
Surprise Lamb
(page 82)

Little Lychee Pancakes
(page 83)

South-East England

Winning Recipes by Julia Barnett

Guest Cook Thane Prince

Warm Salmon Salad with Pine
Kernels (page 84)

Santa Claus' Surprise Lamb

Julia Barnett

melted butter, for greasing

1 teaspoon Ginger and Orange Sauce

grated rind and juice of 1 orange

4 teaspoons hazelnut oil

1 tablespoon smooth peanut butter

1 tablespoon burghul (bulgar wheat), soaked in boiling water for 10 minutes

2 lean middle neck lamb fillets

1 teaspoon soft brown sugar

1 head chicory

2 teaspoons butter

1 yellow pepper, de-seeded and sliced

½ avocado

salt and pepper, to taste

1 Preheat the oven to Gas Mark 6/200°C/400°F. Cut two heart-shaped pieces of greaseproof paper, about 10–11 inches (25–28 cm) across at their widest point, and brush one side of each with butter.

2 Put the Ginger and Orange Sauce in a bowl and blend in the orange rind, 3 teaspoons hazelnut oil, the peanut butter and salt and pepper to taste. Add the burghul and leave for 20 minutes.

3 Meanwhile, cut the lamb into slices and flatten evenly between two sheets of dampened greaseproof paper, using a meat mallet or rolling pin. Sprinkle with brown sugar and salt and pepper to taste.

4 Remove the outside leaves from the chicory and cut the centre into small pieces. Heat 1 teaspoon butter and the orange juice in a small saucepan and cook the chicory and yellow pepper for 2–3 minutes.

5 Heat the remaining 1 teaspoon butter with 1 teaspoon hazelnut oil in a frying pan, add the lamb slices and cook quickly until browned on both sides.

6 Spoon half the chicory and pepper mixture in the centre of each paper heart and arrange the lamb slices on top. Cover with the burghul mixture. Peel and stone the avocado, slice and arrange on top of the burghul.

7 Fold over the greaseproof paper and seal. Place on a baking sheet and cook in the oven for 15 minutes. Serve in the paper parcels.

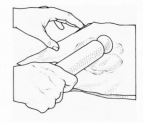

Little Lychee Pancakes

Julia Barnett

For the Pancakes

1 teaspoon vegetable oil

2 oz (50 g) plain flour

pinch of salt

1 egg

¼ pint (150 ml) milk

vegetable oil, for frying

For the Filling

¼ pint (150 ml) Greek yogurt

¼ pint (142 ml) carton double cream

1 tablespoon London or Dutch gin (*genever*)

8 lychees, peeled, halved and stoned

For the Sauce

4 oz (125 g) raspberries

1 oz (25 g) caster sugar

1 To make the pancake batter, put the oil, flour, salt and egg in a bowl and beat well together. Gradually beat in the milk, then leave to stand for 20 minutes.

2 Meanwhile, for the sauce, put the raspberries in a microwave-proof bowl, cover and cook on HIGH (100%) for 3 minutes or until soft, stirring once. (Alternatively, put the raspberries in a heavy-based saucepan and cook over a low heat until soft, breaking down the raspberries with a wooden spoon.) Stir in the caster sugar, then pass through a nylon sieve.

3 Heat a little vegetable oil in a small frying pan and pour in a quarter of the pancake batter, to coat the base of the pan thinly. Cook for 1–2 minutes or until set and golden brown underneath.

4 Toss the pancake or turn with a spatula and cook the second side until golden. Slide on to a plate and set aside. Repeat to make four pancakes.

5 For the filling, whip the yogurt and double cream together until thick, then fold in the gin and lychees. Spread some of the filling on each pancake and fold in half, then in quarters.

6 To serve, spread some raspberry sauce on each of two serving plates and place two filled pancakes on top.

'My special meal is for Thane Prince who inspired me to make pancakes. Normally, her picture in *The Daily Telegraph* makes her look so severe, a bit like Snow White's stepmother. For pancake day, her hair was flying; she looked like she was having so much fun. I like the way her recipes have their theme around special days of the year. My meal is for her to celebrate the Dutch feast of Santa Claus.'

Warm Salmon Salad with Pine Kernels

Thane Prince

8 oz (250 g) skinned and
boned salmon fillet

1 tablespoon olive oil

selection of tiny salad leaves

1 tablespoon pine kernels

½ tablespoon balsamic or red
wine vinegar

1 Slice the salmon into
1 inch (2.5 cm) cubes.

2 Heat the oil in a non-
stick frying pan, add the
salmon and fry for 3–4
minutes or until just
cooked through.

3 Arrange the salad leaves
on two plates and divide
the fish between them.

4 Add the pine kernels to
the oil remaining in the
pan and fry quickly until
lightly browned, then
pour the kernels and the
oil over the fish.

5 Sprinkle each salad with
a few drops of vinegar and
serve at once with fresh
bread.

Julia Barnett is 10 years old and lives in Etchingham, East Sussex. She attends Stonegate School at Wadhurst. Julia was taught to cook by her mother. She also enjoys collecting brass and playing the cello. When she leaves school she would like to train as a cook or a doctor.

Thane Prince writes for *The Daily Telegraph* and other publications. She was made Telegraph Weekend Cook in June 1990 and her first book, *Quick Cook*, was published in July 1991. She is married, has two daughters and lives in London.

Pigeons Wrapped in Lettuce

Thomas Slack (12) from London

2 oven-ready pigeons

2 cos lettuces, trimmed

1 onion, finely chopped

3 tablespoons finely chopped fresh parsley

4–6 fl oz (125–175 ml) red wine

2 oz (50 g) seedless grapes

salt and pepper, to taste

1 Preheat the oven to Gas Mark 5/190°C/375°F.

2 Put the pigeons in a pan of simmering water for 5 minutes, then remove, leave to cool slightly and cut into two using poultry shears.

3 Blanch the lettuces briefly in boiling water. Cut each lengthways into two and sprinkle with chopped onion and 1 tablespoon parsley.

4 Lay a pigeon half on each half of lettuce, tie up firmly with fine string or strong thread and place in a casserole. Warm the wine and pour in enough to come halfway up the sides of the pigeons. Add the grapes and season to taste. Cover and cook in the oven for 40 minutes or until the pigeons are tender.

5 Transfer the pigeons to a warmed serving plate, garnish with the remaining parsley and serve with steamed red cabbage with apple and baked jacket potatoes.

Cod with Coriander in Cream

Judith Rose (15) from Rochester

8 oz (250 g) thick-cut cod fillet, skinned

2 tablespoons plain flour

2 teaspoons ground coriander

2 oz (50 g) butter

1–2 tablespoons lemon juice

1 tablespoon capers

1 egg yolk

6 tablespoons single cream

salt and pepper, to taste

lemon twists, to garnish

1 Divide the fish into two portions. Mix the flour and coriander, season to taste with salt and pepper and use to coat the fish pieces.

2 Heat the butter in a frying pan and fry the fish gently for 3 minutes on each side or until golden, turning once.

3 Add 1 tablespoon lemon juice and the capers to the pan, cover tightly and continue cooking for a further 4–5 minutes or until the fish is tender. Transfer the fish to a warmed serving dish.

4 Beat the egg yolk and cream together, stir into the pan juices and heat gently, without boiling, until thickened. Check the seasoning, adding extra lemon juice if required, and spoon over the fish.

5 Garnish the cod with lemon twists and serve with lightly boiled or steamed broccoli and sauté potatoes.

Crab and Shellfish Supreme

Simon Lyne (13) from West Hoathly

For the Shellfish Supreme

2 large shelled scallops (with shells if possible)

¼ pint (150 ml) dry white wine

2 oz (50 g) butter

¼ onion, finely chopped

2 oz (50 g) mushrooms, sliced

¾ oz (20 g) plain flour

2½ fl oz (65 ml) double cream

1 tablespoon breadcrumbs

salt and pepper, to taste

For the Crab

1 large prepared crab with shell

vinegar or lemon juice, to taste

vegetable oil

salt and pepper, to taste

parsley, to garnish

1 Separate the orange corals from the scallops and reserve. Slice the white parts into rounds and put in a small saucepan with the wine. Poach for about 10 minutes or until tender. Drain, reserving the cooking liquid.

2 Melt 1 oz (25 g) butter in a saucepan, add the onion and mushrooms and cook over a low heat for about 10 minutes. Sprinkle over the flour, then gradually blend in the scallop cooking liquid. Heat gently, stirring constantly, until the sauce thickens.

3 Season the sauce to taste, add half the remaining butter and continue cooking gently for about 6 minutes. Remove from the heat.

4 Preheat the grill until hot. Stir the scallop slices, coral pieces and cream into the sauce and heat through gently, without boiling. Divide the mixture between two buttered scallop shells, if available, or two shallow heatproof serving dishes. Sprinkle with the breadcrumbs, dot with the remaining butter and place under the grill until browned.

5 For the crab, put the dark and white meat in two separate bowls and mix with vinegar or lemon juice and salt and pepper to taste. Neaten the crab shell and rub a little oil inside. Arrange the crab meat inside the shell and garnish with parsley.

6 Serve the crab and shellfish supreme with a mixed green salad and mayonnaise.

Clafoutis

James O'Grady (13) from Ripley

2 whole eggs

1 egg yolk

pinch of salt

2 oz (50 g) caster sugar

2 oz (50 g) plain flour

1 oz (25 g) butter

½ pint (300 ml) milk

½ teaspoon vanilla essence

1 lb (500 g) ripe black cherries, stoned

butter, for greasing

1 Preheat the oven to Gas Mark 4/180°C/350°F. Butter a shallow oven-proof dish.

2 Beat the whole eggs and egg yolks together with the salt until well mixed. Add the sugar and beat until the mixture is light.

3 Gradually sift the flour over the egg mixture, beating vigorously between each addition until the mixture is quite smooth.

4 Melt half the butter over a low heat, taking care not to let it bubble. Incorporate the butter into the egg mixture together with the milk and vanilla essence. Beat well until smooth.

5 Scatter the cherries evenly in the prepared dish and cover with the batter. Dot with the remaining butter and bake in the oven for 45 minutes or until golden and set but still creamy inside. Serve hot or warm.

Zabaglione with Grapes

Emma Hodge (15) from Camberley

Serves Four

9 fl oz (275 ml) medium dry white wine or Marsala

4 oz (125 g) caster sugar

grated rind and juice of ½ lemon

3 egg yolks

1 teaspoon cornflour

2 oz (50 g) black grapes, halved and de-seeded

2 oz (50 g) green grapes, halved and de-seeded

To Decorate

seedless green grapes

1 egg white, lightly whisked

caster sugar

1 To make the frosted grapes for the decoration, dip the grapes in the egg white, then roll them in caster sugar until coated. Leave to dry on grease-proof paper.

2 Mix the wine, sugar, lemon rind, lemon juice, egg yolks and cornflour in a heatproof bowl and place over a saucepan of gently simmering water. Whisk until the mixture becomes frothy. (Do not let the water in the saucepan boil or the mixture will curdle.)

3 Pour the zabaglione into two large serving glasses. Place the halved black and green grapes on top and allow to sink. Decorate the zabaglione with the frosted grapes and serve immediately.

Noodles with Tomato Concasse

Thomas Slack chose Anton Mosimann as his guest cook because he thought he would enjoy the unusual flavours. Anton Mosimann is renowned worldwide for his outstanding career as a Chef de Cuisine. This simple starter would be ideal served before Thomas's Pigeons Wrapped in Lettuce (page 86).

Serves Four

¾ oz (20 g) shallot, finely chopped

1 garlic clove

2¼ lb (1 kg) ripe tomatoes, peeled, de-seeded and chopped into small pieces

few sprigs fresh oregano and thyme

salt and pepper, to taste

1 Sweat the shallot and whole clove of garlic well, without colouring, in a large non-stick pan.

2 Add the chopped tomatoes and herbs and season with salt and pepper.

3 Cover and cook carefully for about 15 minutes until soft and all the liquid has evaporated.

4 Remove the garlic clove and herbs and, if necessary, season again with salt and pepper. Serve over bowls of boiled egg noodles.

Courgettes and Tomatoes au Gratin

Simon Lyne chose Delia Smith as his guest cook because she likes seafood. Delia is the author of many best-selling cookery books and has made frequent television appearances, including presenting her own BBC series, Delia Smith's Cookery Course. Delia suggested this recipe as a good starter to serve before Simon's Crab and Shellfish Supreme (page 88).

4 courgettes, thinly sliced

4 tablespoons olive oil

1 large garlic clove, crushed

4 large tomatoes, skinned and sliced

4 tablespoons grated Parmesan cheese

1 rounded teaspoon dried oregano

4 oz (125 g) Cheddar cheese, grated

salt and pepper, to taste

1 Preheat the oven to Gas Mark 5/190°C/375°F.

2 Put the sliced courgettes in a colander, sprinkling each layer with salt. Place a plate on top, weight this down and leave for 30 minutes. Dry the courgettes with kitchen paper.

3 Heat the oil in a frying pan large enough to hold the courgettes in a single layer (or cook them in batches). Add the courgettes and garlic to the pan and fry until nicely browned.

4 Arrange layers of courgettes and tomatoes in an ovenproof gratin dish, sprinkling each layer with Parmesan cheese, oregano, salt and pepper. Finish with a layer of tomatoes and cover with the grated Cheddar cheese.

5 Bake the gratin on a high shelf in the oven for 30 minutes. Serve with crusty wholemeal bread and butter.

Sainsbury's Young Cook of Britain 1990

Recipes by Gill Nutter

Twelve-year-old Gill Nutter lives in Prestwich, Manchester and attends Prestwich High School. She was Sainsbury's Young Cook of Britain in 1990, but cookery is not her only hobby. After finishing her homework, Gill plays golf at Prestwich Golf Club, often winning prizes there too!

Gill's sister, Susanne, has also won a place in the Sainsbury's Young Cook of Britain competition in previous years, and her brother, Andrew, has just completed a chef's apprenticeship at London's Savoy Hotel.

Chicken in a Tangy Sauce
(Illustrated on the cover)

Gill Nutter (12) from Prestwich

2 skinned chicken breast fillets

1 oz (25 g) carrot

1 oz (25 g) courgette

vegetable oil, for frying

6 leaves lollo rosso lettuce

6 leaves frisée

6 watercress sprigs

4 chives, to garnish

For the Dressing

1 tablespoon red wine vinegar

½ teaspoon Dijon mustard

1 garlic clove, crushed

1 oz (25 g) caster sugar

Worcestershire sauce, to taste

Tabasco sauce, to taste

2 tablespoons olive oil

1 tablespoon soy sauce

1 tablespoon tomato ketchup

salt and pepper, to taste

1 To make the dressing, whisk all the ingredients together.

2 Cut the chicken into strips. Cut the carrot and courgette into fine strips, blanch briefly in boiling water, then drain.

3 Heat a little oil in a frying pan, add the chicken and fry for 10-15 minutes. Remove from the pan, drain on kitchen paper, then keep warm.

4 Arrange the lettuce, frisée and watercress decoratively on two plates and sprinkle with some of the dressing.

5 Put the remaining dressing in a saucepan and heat gently. Add the chicken and vegetables and toss to coat. Pile in the centre of the leaves on the plates. Garnish with chives and serve at once.

Exotic Fruit Flans on a Raspberry Coulis

Gill Nutter

1 egg

1 oz (25 g) caster sugar

1 oz (25 g) plain flour

2 tablespoons Kirsch

2 tablespoons lemon curd

2 oz (50 g) fromage frais

mixed exotic fruits
(eg. kumquats, kiwi fruit, Cape gooseberries, star fruit and grapes), prepared as necessary

For the Raspberry Coulis

3 oz (75 g) raspberries

1 oz (25 g) caster sugar

1 tablespoon water

For the Glaze

3 fl oz (75 ml) water

lemon juice, to taste

1 teaspoon arrowroot

½ oz (15 g) caster sugar

1 Preheat the oven to Gas Mark 5/190°C/375°F. Grease two individual tart or flan tins.

2 Whisk the egg and sugar together until pale and thick. Sift over half the flour and fold in carefully, then sift and fold in the remaining flour. Spoon the mixture into the prepared tins and bake in the oven for 15–20 minutes or until golden brown and springy to the touch.

3 Turn the sponges out on to a wire rack and sprinkle with Kirsch while still hot. Leave to cool.

4 To make the raspberry coulis, put the raspberries, sugar and water in a saucepan and heat gently until soft, breaking up the raspberries with a wooden spoon. Pass through a nylon sieve and leave to cool.

5 Stir the lemon curd into the fromage frais and spread over the sponges. Arrange the fruit on top.

6 Put all the glaze ingredients in a saucepan and bring to the boil, stirring constantly, until thick and clear. Brush carefully over the fruit and leave to cool.

7 To serve, pour the raspberry coulis on to two serving plates and place the flans carefully in the centre.

Index to Recipes

Acknowledgments

Design: Barry Löwenhoff
Illustrations: John Woodcock
Photography: Tim Imrie
Stylist: Anna Tait
Home Economist: Mandy Wagstaff
Coordination: Jane Barker
Typesetting: Goodfellow & Egan, Cambridge
Printed and bound by Printer Trento, Italy

The publishers are also grateful for
permission to reproduce recipes from
the following:
Delia Smith's Complete Cookery Course, British Broadcasting Corporation, 1982
Table Talk with Tovey, Macdonald & Co Ltd, 1981
New Classic Cuisine, the Roux Brothers, Macdonald & Co Ltd, 1983
Ruth Mott's Favourite Recipes, British Broadcasting Corporation, 1990
Take Six More Cooks, Kay Avila, Macdonald & Co Ltd – A Channel 4 Book, 1988
Floyd on France, British Broadcasting Corporation, 1987
A Passion for Mushrooms, Antonio Carluccio, Pan Books, 1989
Le Manoir aux Quat' Saisons, Raymond Blanc, Macdonald & Co Ltd, 1988